D0643615

Infant/Toddler Caregiving

A Guide to Language Development and Communication

Edited by J. Ronald Lally, Peter L. Mangione,

and Carol Lou Young-Holt

Developed by the

Center for Child and Family Studies

Far West Laboratory for Educational Research and Development

for the

Child Development Division

California Department of Education

NATIONAL UNIVERSITY
LIBRARY SACRAMENTO

the Program
for
infant
toddler
caregivers

Publishing Information

Infant/Toddler Caregiving: A Guide to Language Development and Communication was developed by the Center for Child and Family Studies, Far West Laboratory for Educational Research and Development, San Francisco. (See the Acknowledgments on page vi for the names of those who made significant contributions to this document.) The document was edited for publishing by Sheila Bruton, working in cooperation with Peter L. Mangione, Janet L. Poole, and Mary Smithberger. It was prepared for photo-offset production by the staff of the Bureau of Publications, California Department of Education, under the direction of Theodore R. Smith. The layout and cover were designed by Steve Yee, assisted by Juan Sanchez and Lupe Villegas, and typesetting was done by Jeannette I. Huff.

The guide was published by the California Department of Education, 721 Capitol Mall, Sacramento, California (mailing address: P.O. Box 944272, Sacramento, CA 94244-2720). It was distributed under the provisions of the Library Distribution Act and *Government Code* Section 11096.

Copyright © 1992 by the California Department of Education

ISBN 0-8011-0880-2

Ordering Information

Copies of this publication are available for $8.25 each, plus sales tax for California residents, from the Bureau of Publications, Sales Unit, California Department of Education, P.O. Box 271, Sacramento, CA 95812-0271. Other publications that are available from the Department may be found on page 67, or a complete list may be obtained by writing to the address given above or by calling the Sales Unit at (916) 445-1260.

Photo Credits

The California Department of Education gratefully acknowledges the following individuals for the use of the photos that appear in this publication: Sheila Signer, cover, pp. vii, 5, 6, 7, 8, 14, 16, 17, 18, 20, 21, 22, 23, 28, 30, 31, 32, 33, 34, 42, 44, 46, 47, 48, 57, 59, 60, 61, 62; Carol Wheeler, pp. 2, 56.

Contents

Preface

At a time when half the mothers in the United States are gainfully employed, most of them full time, more young children require care outside the home than ever before. The growth of child care services has failed to keep pace with the rapidly increasing demand, making appropriate care for young children difficult for families to find. Training is needed to increase the number of quality child care programs, yet the traditional systems for training child care providers are overburdened. In response to this crisis, the California Department of Education's Child Development Division has developed an innovative and comprehensive approach to training infant and toddler caregivers, called The Program for Infant/Toddler Caregivers. The program is a comprehensive training system consisting of a document entitled *Visions for Infant/Toddler Care: Guidelines for Professional Caregiving,* an annotated guide to media training materials for caregivers, a series of training videotapes, and a series of caregivers' guides.

The purpose of the caregivers' guides is to offer information based on current theory, research, and practice to caregivers in both centers and family child care homes. Each guide addresses an area of infant development and care, covering major issues of concern and related practical considerations. The guides are intended to be used hand in hand with the program's series of videos; the videos illustrate key concepts and caregiving techniques for a specific area of care, and the guides provide extensive and in-depth coverage of a topic.

This guide was written by seven noted experts in the field of early language development and communication. Like the other guides in the series, this one is rich in practical guidelines and suggestions. The information and ideas presented in this document focus on supporting language development and communication in young, mobile, and older infants and becoming sensitive to the vital role of the children's home language and culture in the early development and care of children.

ROBERT W. AGEE
Deputy Superintendent
Field Services Branch

ROBERT A. CERVANTES
Director
Child Development Division

JANET POOLE
Assistant Director
Child Development Division

Acknowledgments

This publication was developed by the Center for Child and Family Studies, Far West Laboratory for Educational Research and Development, under the direction of J. Ronald Lally. Special thanks go to Jacqueline Sachs, Donna J. Thal, Kathleen McCartney, Wendy Wagner Robeson, Eugene E. Garcia, Maria Eugenia Matutue-Bianchi, Janet Gonzalez-Mena, Peter L. Mangione, and Carol Lou Young-Holt, for their contributions of sections to this document; Kathleen Bertolucci, for editorial assistance; and Robert Cervantes, Francis Louie, Mario Muniz, Janet Poole, Mary Smithberger, and Kay Witcher, Child Development Division, California Department of Education, for review and recommendations on content. Thanks are also extended to the members of the national and California review panels for their comments and suggestions. The national panel members were T. Berry Brazelton, Laura Dittman, Richard Fiene, Magda Gerber, Asa Hilliard, Alice Honig, Jeree Pawl, Sally Provence, Eleanor Szanton, Yolanda Torres, Bernice Weissbourd, and Donna Wittmer. The California panel members were Dorlene Clayton, Dee Cuney, Ronda Garcia, Jacquelyne Jackson, Lee McKay, Janet Nielsen, Pearlene Reese, Maria Ruiz, June Sale, Patty Siegel, and Lenore Thompson. Material that appears in the section "From Vision to Practice" was drawn from the Child Development Associate (CDA) Competency Standards for Infant/Toddler Caregivers and Family Day Caregivers. Finally, the "Developmental Milestones" in Sections One and Two are excerpts from *Developmentally Appropriate Practice in Early Childhood Programs Serving Children from Birth Through Age 8,* edited by Sue Bredekamp, copyright © 1987 by the National Association for the Education of Young Children; used by permission.

Introduction

The following pages contain a wealth of information specifically written to help caregivers with their day-to-day efforts to support the language development and communication of infants and toddlers and their families. This caregivers' guide, one of a series developed by The Program for Infant/Toddler Caregivers, is a companion document to *Visions for Infant/Toddler Care: Guidelines for Professional Caregiving.*

The California Department of Education created *Visions* to outline guidelines for quality care for children under three years of age. *Visions* covers all the major caregiving domains, from providing a safe and healthy learning environment to establishing supportive relationships with families. This guide deals with Vision VII: Developing Each Child's Competence—Language Development.

The guide is divided into five sections. In the first three sections, nationally recognized experts approach the question of how caregivers can support early language development and communication in young, mobile, and older infants. Sections Four and Five, also written by nationally acclaimed experts, discuss the impact of bilingualism and culture on the early development of language and communication by the infant and toddler. All five sections close with specific points to consider, a list of appropriate practices for caregivers, and suggested resources for further information on the section's topic.

Each section focuses on either a particular developmental period or the impact of culture on early language development and communication. The guide underscores the importance of providing flexible and individualized caregiving based on both the child's developmental level and the family's linguistic and cultural heritage. Such caregiving provides an enriched, supportive environment for language development and communication based on responsive, trust-building relationships with the child and the family.

Language Development: Vision Statement

The caregiver actively communicates with children and provides opportunities and support for children to understand, acquire, and use verbal and nonverbal means of communicating thoughts and feelings.

Communication between people can take many forms, including spoken words or sounds, gestures, eye and body movements, and touch. Children need to understand both verbal and nonverbal means of communicating thoughts, feelings, and ideas. Adults can help children develop such skills by encouraging communication and providing ample opportunity for children to listen, interact, and express themselves freely with other children and adults. . . . Successful caregivers of infants and toddlers appreciate cultures, customs, languages, and child-rearing practices different from the caregivers' own. . . .

Young infants need adults who are attentive to their individual signals. Sensitive responsiveness to vocal messages encourages communication. Infants' early babblings and cooings are important practice for later verbal expression. Their speech development is facilitated by an encouraging partner who responds to their beginning communications, repeats their sounds, offers sounds for them to imitate, and explains events to the baby while they are taking place.

Mobile infants begin to jabber expressively, name familiar objects and people, and understand many words and phrases. Adults can build on this communication by showing active interest in children's expressions, interpreting their first attempts at words, repeating and expanding on what they say, talking to them clearly, and telling simple stories.

Toddlers daily increase their vocabularies and use of sentences. There is a wide range of normal language development during this time. Adults can communicate actively with all toddlers—modeling good speech, listening to them carefully, making use of and expanding on what they say, and helping them with new words and phrases. Language can be used in a variety of pleasurable ways each day—through songs, stories, directions, comfort, conversations, information, and play.[1]

---

[1] This statement is an excerpt from Vision VII: Developing Each Child's Competence, with an insert adapted from the Introduction to Visions for Infant/Toddler Caregivers, in *Visions for Infant/Toddler Care: Guidelines for Professional Caregiving* (Sacramento: California Department of Education, 1988).

From Vision to Practice

The infant/toddler caregiver working in a center or family child care home can act to support the vision of language development and communication by:

1. Listening and talking with children
   The caregiver:
   - Talks often with individual children and stimulates conversation among them and with adults in the center or home.
   - Is aware of the caregiver's role as a language model for children and uses affectionate and playful tones, clear speech, and responsive conversation.
   - Listens attentively to children, tries to understand what they want to communicate, and helps them express themselves.
   - Talks with children about special experiences and relationships in their families and home lives.

2. Providing appropriate activities
   The caregiver:
   - Helps children connect word meaning(s) to experiences and real objects.
   - Uses a variety of songs, stories, books, and games (including those from the children's cultures) for language development.

3. Evaluating language development
   The caregiver:
   - Has realistic expectations for each child's understanding and use of speech based on knowledge of language development and the individual child.
   - Recognizes, understands, and respects local speech patterns and idioms.

4. Encouraging the use of the child's home language
   The caregiver:
   - Respects the language of non-English-speaking families and encourages them to communicate freely with their children in the language parents prefer.
   - Supports non-English-speaking and bilingual children's attempts to develop and use the home language as much as possible.

5. Communicating with parents
   The caregiver:
   - Shares children's communication/language achievements with parents on a daily basis.
   - Seeks information from parents about their child's language and communication development in the home environment.
   - Helps parents find opportunities to learn English, if requested.

6. Recognizing special needs
   The caregiver:
   - Recognizes possible impairments or delays that affect hearing and speech, helps families find resources, cooperates with treatment plans, and finds ways to communicate positively with children who have hearing or speech impairments.

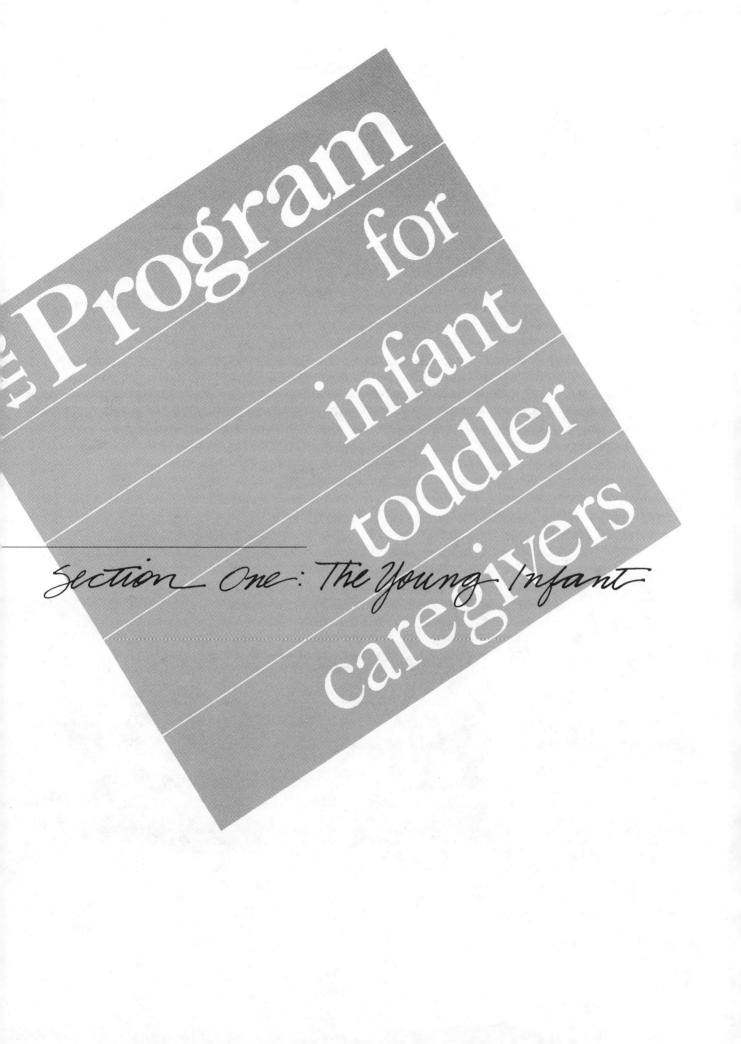

The Program for infant toddler caregivers

Section One: The Young Infant

Introduction

n this section Jacqueline Sachs describes in detail the early language development of the young infant from birth to six months and the role of the caregiver in providing an environment supportive of language and communication needs.

Jacqueline Sachs is Professor of Communication Sciences, Psychology, and Linguistics at the University of Connecticut. She has written numerous papers on language development and teaches courses on normal language acquisition to students in speech–language pathology and education. Among Dr. Sachs's interests is communication during the first year of life, which was the subject of a chapter she recently contributed to Jean Berko Gleason's textbook *The Development of Language*.

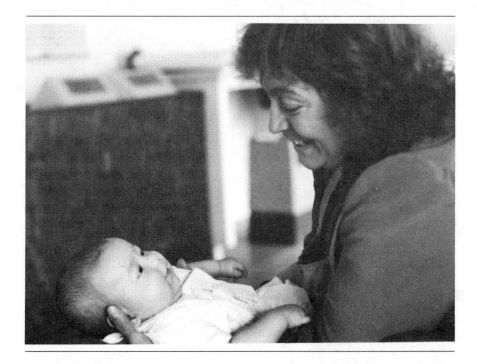

Emergence of Communication: Earliest Signs

Jacqueline Sachs

Between birth and six months of age, infants may seem completely helpless, but they are already communicating with caregivers in many fascinating ways. One of the infants' first and most important abilities is that of getting the caregiver's attention. How the babies are responded to and encouraged to communicate is important for later language development. This chapter examines how infants perceive the world around them, what communicative messages they produce, and how you as a caregiver can best interact with babies.

The Infant's Perceptual Abilities

Many people think newborns cannot see or hear. However, in addition to being able to feel, taste, and smell, the newborn can see and hear remarkably well.

Ability to See

Newborns see best at a distance of about 8 to 15 inches, the distance at which your face will be when you are feeding or playing with newborn infants. Babies look at what they like, and what they like best at birth is the human face. Watch the baby's face and eyes; they will tell you whether the baby is interested in interacting or wants to be alone.

Ability to Hear

Recent research has shown that babies hear sounds, such as their mother's voice and heartbeat, even *before* the babies are born. Newborns not only can hear sounds, they are especially fascinated with the human voice. Infants are equipped to hear all the sounds that would be used in any language spoken by any people anywhere in the world.

It is important that infants hear lots of language in the first year of life because in the absence of speech sounds, the brain areas for the perception of speech do not develop normally. Researchers discovered that by one year of age babies begin to lose the ability to discriminate sounds they do not hear in the language spoken around them (Werker and Tees 1984). For example, in a study of babies who were exposed only to English, the researchers found that infants between six and eight months of age could discriminate sounds used, not in English, but in Hindi or Salish. By ten to twelve months of age, that ability had disappeared. Therefore, the period often called "prelinguistic" (or "before language") clearly is not prelinguistic. Some important learning is taking place.

Communicative Messages

Nature has equipped infants with two major strategies to get the caregiver's attention. The first is crying. Because cries are noisy and generally unpleasant to listen to, we are motivated to figure out what is wrong so the infant will stop crying. Second, infants are cute and do cute things, such as cooing, babbling, and making funny faces. This cuteness draws us to infants and makes us want to interact with them.

Crying

Although crying in a young infant is not deliberate communication, it does serve as the first communicative message to the caregiver. Many experts suggest that by responding to the baby's cries, you are allowing the baby to learn at an early age that communication is possible and useful. The sounds made by the baby while he or she is crying become more differentiated as the infant gets older. As you get to know an individual baby, you may be able to interpret the cry as meaning "I'm hungry," "I'm hurting," or "I'm tired."

Cooing

These pleasant sounds (something like "oooo") are the earliest sounds made as a result of friendly social interaction. They often emerge at about two months of age (Stark 1979), but there is considerable individual variation among babies. Infants are delighted when you talk or "oooo" back to them.

Babbling

Most infants begin babbling at about six months of age. Babbling indicates that the infants are experimenting with the feelings and sounds of their voices. Babies babble both socially and when alone. Like unresponsiveness to speech sounds, the absence of babbling may be a warning sign, although babies vary considerably in how much they babble.

The presence of babbling is not a guarantee that a baby's hearing is normal because deaf babies also begin to babble. Their babbling usually begins somewhat later than that of hearing babies, and eventually the deaf baby's babbling drops off (Oller and Eilers 1988). Therefore, it is important for caregivers to pay careful attention if an infant's babbling stops. If that happens, have the infant's hearing checked for potential hearing loss or inability to hear.

Nonverbal Communication

In addition to making sounds, the young infant communicates with the face and body. The baby's ever-changing facial expressions and body movements can tell a great deal about the baby's needs and moods. The actions are part of the baby's communication at this early age.

As a caregiver you should be aware that there are differences in the ways various cultural groups interact with young infants and that those differences may be reflected in the way the infant interacts with you. For example, some babies live in an environment with almost constant human contact; babies are held, cuddled, passed from person to person, and carried about (Heath 1983). In such a setting, a lot of nonverbal communication is part of the close physical contact between the baby and the caregivers. It would not be surprising if an infant from such a culture were to be distressed at not being held in a child care setting. The infant might have a rich repertoire of nonverbal communication, but this repertoire has developed in a specific cultural setting and might not be displayed when the setting is different. Section Five, "Culture, Communication, and the Care of Infants and Toddlers," provides more information on cultural differences in infant care.

Interaction with Young Infants

Although much of what a child care provider does involves groups of children, it is important that the caregiver's interaction with the infant less than six months old be on a one-to-one basis. It is crucial that each baby, not just the most demanding ones, get some of your undivided attention. There are two aspects to interaction: stimulating communication and responding to communicative attempts. Stimulation can be thought of as what you do on your own initiative and your responsiveness, how you respond when the baby initiates an interaction.

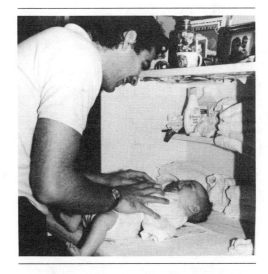

Stimulating Communication

In an earlier section, The Infant's Perceptual Abilities, the importance of infants hearing speech in the first year of life was pointed out. But one might ask, How much speech and what sort of speech? The answer depends on both the infant's current state and the infant's temperament.

Learn to judge the infant's state and rhythm of transition from one state to another. All babies vary from time to time in how ready they are for interaction, depending on their current state (for example, fully alert and ready for play, awake but not alert, drowsy, or sleeping). In *Born Dancing* the authors describe the fully alert state: "All the fascinating dialogue dances you and your baby share take place during this fun-filled state. Your baby may coo, grunt, and make other contented sounds as he looks at you, tries to make eye contact, and invites you to play. Enjoy it!" (Thoman and Browder 1987, 149).

Babies also need rest and quiet times. Their state constantly changes, so you, the caregiver, must be able to assess the infant's present state. However, do not be overly concerned about doing something inappropriate.

One expert on the interactional patterns of caregivers and infants has suggested that occasional "messing up" (behaving in a way that is inappropriate for the infant's current state) is potentially a stimulus for growth (Stern 1977). Infants learn that their caregivers are responsive to them, but they also learn to cope when the caregivers are not responsive.

Take the infant's temperament into consideration in choosing how stimulating or soothing your interaction should be. For more information about temperament, refer to the article by Stella Chess in *Infant/Toddler Caregiving: A Guide to Social–Emotional Growth and Socialization* and to the video *Flexible, Fearful, or Feisty: The Different Temperaments of Infants and Toddlers*. The "easy" infant may be able to handle highly stimulating interaction, whereas the "difficult" infant may need a more soothing approach. The "slow-to-warm-up" infant may need to be approached first in a soothing way, but later the infant may respond happily to stimulating play. Again, however, beware of categorizing a baby by temperament type. These types exist on a continuum, and for appropriate communicative interaction, you need to get to know each baby individually. Learn to judge when and what kind of stimulation brings out the best in each baby.

When infants are in a mood to interact, be attentive to them. This mutual attending is the beginning of communication, and later language development rests on establishing such patterns during the earlier stages. Do not be only a caregiver; be a playmate as well. You may think it does not matter whether you talk to such young babies when they cannot understand your words, but the "music" of your voice is more important than the words (Stern 1977).

Use baby talk. This recommendation may surprise you because in our culture the term "baby talk" has some negative connotations. We think of it as saying only things like "tummy" for "stomach" or "choo-choo" for "train." Some people say they never use baby talk to young children. If you listen to those people, however, they certainly do not talk to an infant or young child the same way they talk to an adult. If they did, they would definitely not hold the child's attention for very long. I am using the term "baby talk" in its broader sense, that is, as speech modified to be interesting and understandable to young children. This sort of baby talk is indeed appropriate for a baby.

Special ways of speaking to infants and young children are found in all cultures and have similar features almost

everywhere. Baby talk has a generally higher pitch with more overall variation in pitch (some words very high and some very low), dramatic variations in loudness (even whispers often hold the baby's attention), and an exaggerated stress on words that forms a regular rhythmic pattern. Baby talk does hold infants' attention better than adult-to-adult speech does. Anne Fernald (1985) played tapes of women talking with and without baby-talk characteristics to four-month-old infants. The babies could select which tape to hear simply by turning their heads toward one of the speakers. The babies consistently preferred the voice using baby talk.

Fortunately, you do not have to *learn* how to talk baby talk. An expert on baby talk believes adults have an inborn ability to teach language, just as babies have an inborn ability to learn it (Bernstein Ratner 1984). If you pay attention to the baby's reactions, you will use baby talk quite naturally—especially if you do not worry about sounding silly to another adult.

Have an expressive face as well as an expressive voice. Exaggerated expressions like surprise or frowns go along with baby talk. Daniel Stern (1977) found that eye contact is held much longer in interaction with infants than with adults. The primary reason for using baby talk, exaggerated facial expressions, and prolonged eye contact is that they hold the infant's attention and thus help you and the baby get to know each other as individuals (Sachs 1988).

The first messages you convey will be emotional ones. *What* you say does not matter, but how you say it and what you really feel when you say it do matter. When your emotions are not positive, your real feelings have a way of "leaking" through in your voice and face. If you say, "You're my sweetie pie," but you feel bored and irritable, the negative messages will probably be the ones that come through. Similarly, you communicate best when you are not distant and "professional" but emotionally involved with each and every baby.

Responding to Communicative Attempts

In addition to providing stimulation, caregivers should respond to the baby's initiations. Infants seek communication; by responding to the infant, you provide important lessons about communication from a very early age. Long before the first word is uttered, and even well before the first word is understood, the infant has learned a great deal about how language works. You are teaching three lessons as you respond to infants:

Lesson 1: Communication matters. One of the first communicative lessons caregivers teach infants is "People will pay attention to you when you try to communicate." Acknowledge the baby's subtle behavioral cues and bids for attention. Authors Evelyn Thoman and Sue Browder (1987, 161) describe how caring adults enter into a "dance" with the baby that makes the baby feel loved and in tune with others.

When the baby smiles, coos, waves his or her hands, or otherwise tries to attract your attention, you probably respond naturally by nodding, smiling, or talking. By paying attention to the baby's subtle cues much of the time, you are helping the infant learn about the world. Anything you do to let the baby know you have noticed the bid for attention, such as laughing, talking, smiling, or responding with an animated facial expression, helps that child feel important and loved.

Keep in mind that infants differ in how much they initiate interaction so that you do not give less time to the relatively passive infant who does not demand attention. Do not worry about "spoiling" a young infant who is more demanding. You want to give all infants a sense that they can affect their environment and that they are loved.

Lesson 2: People take turns communicating. The next lesson the infant learns

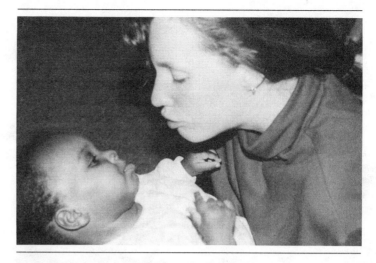

is "Sometimes I talk and you listen; sometimes you talk and I listen." Studies conducted of adults and babies while they are communicating show that the babies realize very early that communication involves taking turns (Snow 1977). An infant first becomes aware of turn taking when the caregiver *gives* the baby a turn. For example, Catherine Snow videotaped mothers interacting with babies three months of age. She found that the mothers left spaces in their vocalizations for the infants' turns and accepted anything the children did (a smile, a coo, or even a burp) as a conversational turn. The following is one example of a "conversation" between a mother and her three-month-old daughter, Ann (Snow 1977, 12):

Ann: (Smiles)
Mother: "Oh, what a nice little smile! Yes, isn't that nice? There. There's a nice little smile."
Ann: (Burps)
Mother: "What a nice wind as well! Yes, that's better, isn't it? Yes. Yes. Yes!"
Ann: (Vocalizes)
Mother: "That's a nice noise."

What mothers accepted as turns changed over time. The mothers of older infants began to ignore things like burps and to respond only to babblings as a turn.

Turn taking is a good way to avoid overstimulating a young infant because you leave space for responses and pay attention to those responses. You want the baby to learn to be an *active* conversational partner.

Lesson 3: Sounds are an important part of routines. Infants begin to learn language through the repeated use of sounds or words in routines and rituals. Although most babies will not begin to speak until they are about a year old, they begin much earlier to expect certain sounds in certain contexts. To begin to break into the complex code that language is, babies need consistent pairings of sounds with objects and activities.

One source of these pairings is in baby games. Some standard games (for example, "peek-a-boo," "I'm gonna get you," and "give-and-take") are found many places in the world. Although the caregiver may think of these games as only play, infants learn by playing them.

Individual, invented games are just as important and useful in interacting with babies. Any playful thing you repeat can become your game with that baby. Even during the first six months of life, the baby will gradually learn what to expect in the game. The particular sounds or words in your games are not important—they may be "moo," for what the cow says; or "so big," in the game of "How big is baby?" or "boop," with a touch on the nose. What is happening is that the baby is being given the chance to realize that a sound goes with a situation.

Do not expect the six-month-old infant to be able to imitate these sounds or produce them spontaneously. Usually, signs that the baby has expectations about sounds in routine situations do not emerge until the second half of the first year. The first use of language typically emerges in these routine situations. By nine months of age, the baby will probably understand some words, and by a year, begin to speak. But the baby has been preparing for those steps from the beginning, during the important first six months of interaction with loving, responsive caregivers.

Warning Signs

A general lack of interest in social contact is a warning sign. For example, the baby who never looks at your eyes when you attempt to make eye contact, or the baby who holds his or her body rigidly when in your arms, is not engaging in social interaction typical of young infants.

Notice also whether the infant attends to your speech. If a baby seems inattentive to the human voice, even when reactive to other loud noises, there is reason for concern. Speech sounds occur within a particular frequency range, and hearing within this range is necessary for normal language development. There are two possible reasons for inattention to the human voice:

1. If the baby does not seem to notice when people are talking to him or her, this may be a sign of a chronic hearing impairment. An assessment of the baby's hearing by an audiologist is possible even in the first six months of life. Hearing testing is highly recommended if the baby seems unresponsive to speech; early intervention is possible and crucial for the child's normal language development.

2. Many babies develop ear infections or fluid in their ears because of respiratory infections. Sometimes it is

obvious that something is wrong because the infant cries from the pain and may have a fever. Medical attention is necessary to combat the ear infection. However, many babies may seem to be well but nevertheless develop fluid in their ears that interferes with their hearing. Therefore, it is very important that you notice whether an infant responds normally to you when you speak. If you suspect that a baby has become inattentive to speech, appropriate medical evaluation and intervention are imperative. Even temporary hearing problems caused by fluid in the ear, if the problems occur frequently, can have a long-term effect on language development.

References

Bernstein Ratner, N. "How We Talk to Children: Its Theoretical and Clinical Implications," *Journal of the National Student Speech-Language-Hearing Association*, Vol. 11, No. 1 (1984), 33–45.

Fernald, Anne. "Four-Month-Old Infants Prefer to Listen to Motherese," *Infant Behavior and Development,* Vol. 8 (1985), 181–195.

Heath, Shirley B. *Ways with Words: Language, Life and Work in Communities and Classrooms.* New York: Cambridge University Press, 1983.

Oller, D. K., and R. E. Eilers. "The Role of Audition in Infant Babbling," *Child Development,* Vol. 59 (1988), 441–449.

Sachs, Jacqueline. "Communication Development in Infancy," in *The Development of Language* (Second edition). Edited by Jean Berko Gleason. Columbus, Ohio: Merrill Publishing Co., 1988.

Snow, Catherine. "The Development of Conversation Between Mothers and Babies," *Journal of Child Language,* Vol. 4 (1977), 1–22.

Stark, R. E. "Prespeech Segmental Feature Development," in *Language Acquisition: Studies in First Language Development.* Edited by Paul Fletcher and Michael Garman. New York: Cambridge University Press, 1979.

Stern, Daniel. *The First Relationship: Infant and Mother.* Developing Child Series. Edited by Jerome Bruner and others. Cambridge, Mass.: Harvard University Press, 1977.

Thoman, Evelyn B., and Sue Browder. *Born Dancing: The Relaxed Parents' Guide to Making Babies Smart with Love.* New York: Harper & Row Pubs., Inc., 1987.

Werker, J., and R. C. Tees. "Cross-language Speech Perception: Evidence for Perceptual Reorganization During the First Year of Life," *Infant Behavior and Development*, Vol. 7 (1984), 49–64.

Developmental Milestones

The following developmental milestones are approximations at best. It is important to remember that there are great individual differences among children and that early language mastery is not necessarily associated with later language mastery. These milestones come from *Developmentally Appropriate Practice in Early Childhood Programs Serving Children from Birth Through Age 8.*

The infant:

- Cries to signal pain or distress.
- Smiles or vocalizes to initiate social contact.
- Responds to human voices. Gazes at faces.
- Uses vocal and nonvocal communication to express interest and exert influence.
- Babbles, using all types of sounds. Engages in private conversations when alone.

- Combines babbles. Understands names of familiar people and objects. Laughs. Listens to conversations.

Points to Consider

1. Are you responding to all the infant's communicative attempts (crying, cooing, babbling, and facial expressions) in a way that is sensitive to the infant's state of activity *or* inactivity and the infant's temperament? For example, caregivers need to be sensitive to infants' activity states, providing stimulation when the infants are fully alert and allowing a quiet, peaceful time when they are not.
2. Are you giving all infants the special, individual attention they require to have their needs met and to develop normal language and communication skills?
3. Are you "dancing" with infants when they make a bid for your attention by crying, cooing, waving an arm, or making a face?
4. Are you taking turns with the baby by waiting your turn and responding after the infant has communicated?
5. Are you providing the babies in your care with a wide range of sounds early in life so that the babies' brain areas for the perception of speech can continue to develop normally?
6. Are you using baby talk as an appropriate way to provide a variety of sounds for infants?
7. Are you noticing whether a baby is uninterested in social communicative contact, in general, and aware that this is a warning sign? For example:
   - If the baby never looks at your eyes when you attempt to make eye contact, holds the body rigidly in your arms, or seems inattentive to the human voice, there is reason for concern.

- It is possible to have a baby's hearing tested by an audiologist even during the first six months of life. This is highly recommended when the baby seems unresponsive to speech because early intervention is crucial if language is to develop normally.

It is important that you mention your concern to the parents so they can bring the problem to the attention of their family doctor, pediatrician, or health-care worker.

Caregiver's Practices

The caregiver working with young infants (birth to six months) can support language development and communication by:

1. Listening and talking with children
   The caregiver:
   - Responds specifically to each infant's cry, trying to learn the meaning of different cries and to respond appropriately (for example, knows when an infant is crying because of hunger, pain, tiredness, and so forth).
   - Responds to the individual infant's cooing and babbling sounds and imitates them, encouraging a "conversation" in which the infant often can take the lead.
   - Talks to infants about what they can see and what is happening during physical routines, such as diapering and feeding.
   - Responds to body signs and nonverbal cues that signal discomfort, excitement, pleasure, and so forth and describes the infant's feeling out loud.
   - Responds sensitively to infants, based on their state and temperament, and encourages infants to interact and attend to the caregiver when the infants are in the mood to do so.

2. Providing appropriate activities
The caregiver:
- Uses baby talk in an expressive voice, with more variation than normally is used with adults or older children (for example, some words are spoken in very high and some in very low pitch); also varies the volume (for example, whispers).
- Sings to infants or uses the voice in interesting ways that encourage listening.
- Uses the face, along with the voice, in expressive ways that encourage the infant to pay attention.
3. Communicating with parents
The caregiver:
- Shares with parents the meaning of an infant's beginning communications, such as different kinds of crying, patterns of temperament, and state of activity or inactivity.
- Encourages parents to share their observations of their infant.

Suggested Resources
Books and Articles

Infant/Toddler Caregiving: A Guide to Social–Emotional Growth and Socialization. Sacramento: California Department of Education, 1990.

Presents information based on current theory, research, and practice on the social–emotional development and socialization of infants and toddlers. Rich in practical guidelines and suggestions for caregivers. Focuses on the caregiver becoming sensitive to the individual needs of infants and toddlers and creating emotionally nurturing relationships with them.

Stern, Daniel. *The First Relationship: Infant and Mother.* Developing Child Series. Edited by Jerome Bruner and others. Cambridge, Mass.: Harvard University Press, 1977.

Considers in detail the importance of the first relationship and the infant's development. Focusing on the first six months, this readable book provides detailed information about the language and communication development of the young infant.

Thoman, Evelyn B., and Sue Browder. *Born Dancing: How Intuitive Parents Understand Their Baby's Unspoken Language and Natural Rhythms.* New York: Harper & Row Pubs., Inc., 1988.

Discusses in a very readable way the interaction and interrelationship between parent and child. For parents and caregivers alike, this book provides a sound child development basis for natural "dancing" with an infant. Different from most parenting books, this one is very supportive and refreshing in its approach.

Zero to Three, Vol. XI, No.1 (September, 1990), 1–26.

Presents a series of articles on the communicative competence of infants and toddlers by writers such as Barry Prizant and Amy Wetherby, Lee McLean, Stanley Greenspan, and Diane Fraser. Topics range from the assessment of communication to intervention approaches with children who have language delays or language disorders.

Audiovisuals

Baby Talk. 1984. Videocassette, color, 49 minutes. Available from Media Guild, 11722 Sorrento Valley Road, Suite E, San Diego, CA 92121; telephone (619) 755-9191.

Examines modern research on child language development from fetal and early infant responses to speech, the innate abilities of language in humans, and the relationship of cognition and language. The film includes interviews with Jerome Bruner, Noam Chomsky, Dan Slobin, Peter Eimas, Catherine Snow, Jean Berko Gleason, Andrew Malzoff, and Eve Clark, all prominent American university linguists.

Benjamin. BBC, Time-Life, Nova Series, 1977. Videocassette (3/4" only), color, 42 minutes. Available from University of Texas at Dallas, Media Center, P.O. Box 830643, Richardson, TX 75083; telephone (214) 690-2949.

A study of an infant's growth and development during the first six months of life, including the infant's ability to recognize his mother, reach for objects, carry on conversations, and influence his parent's behavior toward him. Periodic interviews with Benjamin's parents are interwoven with both film clips of Benjamin's behavior and interaction with his parents and narrative information on the developmental research studying early infancy and infant-parent interaction.

Flexible, Fearful, or Feisty: The Different Temperaments of Infants and Toddlers. Sacramento: California Department of Education, 1990. Video-cassette, color, 29 minutes; printed guide. Videocassette available in English, Spanish, and Chinese (Cantonese).

Illustrates temperamental traits of infants and toddlers and provides caregivers with techniques for dealing with the differences between individual infants and toddlers in a group setting.

Out of the Mouths of Babes. Nature of Things Series, CBS Film K, 1973. Videocassette or 16mm film, color, 28 minutes. Available from Filmmakers Library, 124 E. 40th St., New York, NY 10016; telephone (212) 355-6545.

Provides an overview of chronological development of language in children from infancy to age six. Concentrating on the research of Peter and Jill DeVilliers from Harvard University, the film shows how children seem to learn a language on their own. The film notes the gradual progression from early babbling, gesturing, and one-word sentences to the use of complicated structures and linguistic concepts that extract rules of grammar from the language children hear around them.

Talking to Babies. Los Angeles: California State University, Los Angeles, Division of Special Education, 1989. Videocassette, color, 12 minutes. Available from Mother-Infant Communication Project, California State University, Los Angeles, Division of Special Education, 5151 University Drive, Los Angeles, CA 90032; telephone (213) 343-4414.

Demonstrates ways to talk with younger infants. Discusses the importance of responding to and supporting the infant's early communications.

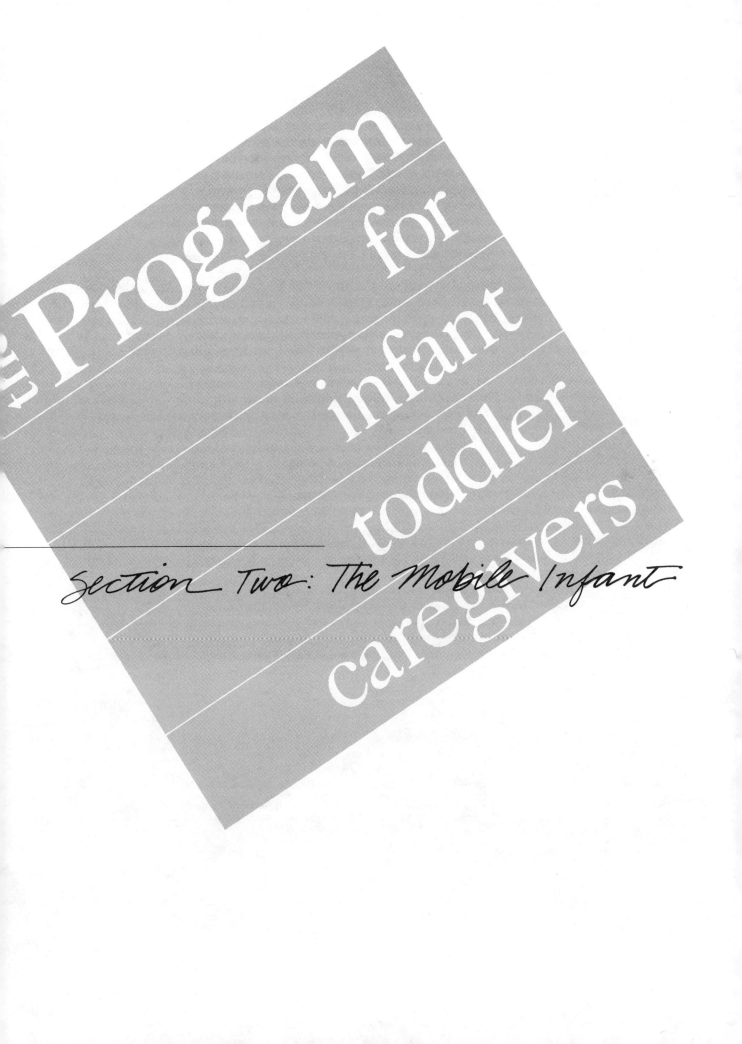

The Program for infant toddler caregivers

Section Two: The Mobile Infant

Introduction

In this section Donna J. Thal describes the important milestones in the language development and communication of the mobile infant. She discusses in detail the concept of "joint reference" (when the baby and the caregiver focus on the same thing and start the first "conversation" about it). Dr. Thal explains how this early conversation supports the infant's developing language.

Donna J. Thal is Associate Professor of Communication Disorders at San Diego State University and a research psychologist at the Center for Research and Language at the University of California at San Diego. Dr. Thal engages in research on language and cognition in the early stages of development. Her current research areas include language and gesture in late talkers and continuity and variation in early language development in early childhood. Dr. Thal has many years of clinical experience with speech/language-impaired children.

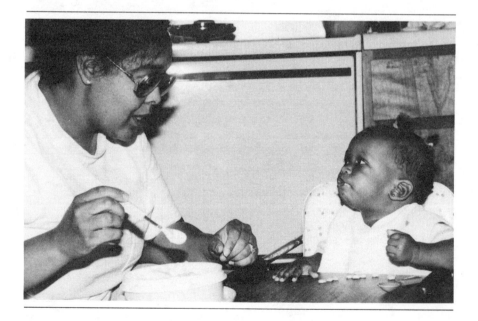

Emergence of Communication: Give-and-Take Between Adult and Child

Donna J. Thal

In the previous section, Jacqueline Sachs showed that by six months of age children have been involved in many important communicative exchanges. Young infants have learned that caregivers respond to their cries by providing the appropriate remedy (for example, a dry diaper, food, or a hug to make them feel secure). As a result, the infants have come to trust the adults who care for them. Because of this early experience, the children are ready for the next steps in the development of communication and language.

Language is the most important mental accomplishment of early childhood. Without the ability to use language skillfully, children are destined to fail in school, which makes them, as adults, less capable of competing successfully for good jobs. Without the ability to use language skillfully, children fail to establish positive relationships with peers and develop a pattern of isolation from social interaction. Thus, the development of language is a critical step in human growth. Between six and sixteen months of age, children take some of the most important steps in learning language, and it is vital that caregivers recognize and reinforce these steps.

The purpose of this section is to help you learn to recognize how infants communicate and the changes in communication that occur in infants between six and sixteen months of age. Once you know what to expect, you will be able to interact with individual children in ways that will foster development of good language and communication.

Although you are responsible for more than one child at a time, remember that children this young cannot function as a group. At least at the beginning of this stage, infants are not aware of things much beyond their immediate reach. Part of the excitement of development in this age range is the infant's transition to mobility, which leads to exploration of larger spaces with more people and things. But the caregiver–child interactions that are most helpful to the child's development during this stage are still one-to-one.

Three important phenomena occur in the infant between six and sixteen months of age, and each contains a number of steps. These developments are (1) the establishment of joint reference to an object or activity with another person (usually an adult caregiver); (2) the onset of intentional communication; and (3) the use of conventional symbols (gestures, vocalizations, and words) to communicate with other people.

Establishment of Joint Reference—Six to Eight Months

By six months of age, the child has developed the physical and sensory distinctions of self and other. This awareness allows the child to master the first of the three phenomena described: establishing joint reference. Joint reference means that two people look at or pay attention to the same thing at the same time. The noted psychologist Daniel Stern has described in detail how mothers and infants reach this point, with particular emphasis on the back-and-forth, your turn–my turn type of interaction that mother and child practice from the early stages (Stern 1985). The establishment of joint reference is another step, along with the earlier turn taking, in the "dance" of communication the child and adult have been developing. In a sense, joint reference is the first way that the topic of a "conversation" is established.

Awareness and Communication at Six Months

By six months of age, normal infants understand the turn-taking game, which they will continue to use in conversation when their language becomes more sophisticated. The infants also understand the rudiments of joint reference; they will observe the direction of the caregiver's gaze, then look in the same direction to find the object being looked at.

Also by the time the infant is six months old, the caregiver and child have developed a number of cues by which they establish joint reference. While caregivers attend to an infant, they often look at objects and vocalize (that is, produce sounds such as "ooo" or words like "look!") as well as change their intonation (such as raise the pitch of the voice).

Establishing joint attention goes in both directions. The six-month-old infant

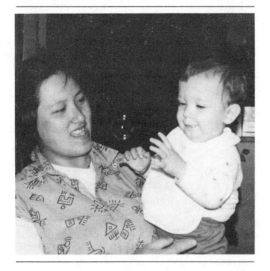

can follow the caregiver's line of sight, but caregivers also monitor the faces of the infants in their care and look at the objects and events to which the infants are attending. Usually, the caregiver also tries to determine exactly what has caught the infant's attention and provide a name for it. Introducing words for what the infant is looking at or playing with is far more effective than trying to teach the infant words in which the infant is not interested at the moment.

While the infant is approximately six through ten months of age, there is continuous refinement in the establishment of joint reference between the caregiver and the infant. The later stages will overlap with the next crucial step: the onset of intentional communication.

Steps in the Development of Joint Reference

The major work on the development and function of joint reference has been carried out by Jerome Bruner. The following descriptions are adapted from his work (Bruner 1983).

In the earliest phases of joint attention, the caregiver simply looks at something nearby, and the infant, after looking at the caregiver's face, looks at the same thing. It may be an object (for example, a toy, stuffed animal, or the infant's crib) or an activity (for example, other children playing with a ball). By paying attention to the same thing at the same time, the infant and caregiver can share the experience of the object or event. That, in turn, allows the caregiver to provide examples of the words that go with the object or event. In this way caregivers expose children to the connection between words and things.

An important change begins when the infant is about six months old. The child's interest in toys and objects increases, shifting away from looking at people's faces to looking at and manipulating objects. This change happens partly because the child's eye–hand coordination has improved, and infants can now reach, grasp, and manipulate the objects that interest them. However, the objects themselves, and sharing them with trusted adults, seem to be of special concern. At this age infants spend a lot of time and effort trying to reach and take objects, to exchange them, and so on. As children become excited about all the new things to be found in the world, the children's interactions with adults become three-way; that is, the interactions include the infant, the caregiver, and some object of interest to the infant.

Although infants have learned that they can share attention to an object or event with another person, they still do not share the activities with any intention to communicate about them. Before six to nine months of age, children may communicate by crying or reaching. Although caregivers interpret children's desires and intervene, children do not realize as they cry that their signals will serve a communicative purpose. The infants' early cries are automatic reactions to some internal feelings.

As children move from automatic to intentional communication (between eight to twelve months of age), the sharing of joint reference changes. When they are about nine months old, children come to understand the meaning of pointing by others. If the caregiver points, the infant will look at the target and not just at the pointing hand (as would have happened earlier). Also at this stage, after looking at the target, the infant will look back at the caregiver, using feedback from the caregiver's face for confirmation that the infant was correct. The caregiver also often names the object to which he or she points.

During this entire period, the caregiver watches the infant's face more than the infant watches the caregiver. This monitoring provides a good model for all caregivers and is a hallmark of caregiver behavior with infants who are eight to sixteen months old. By monitoring the child's glances and signs of interest, the caregiver can interpret the environment for the child—providing the appropriate labels and setting the stage for labeling by the child.

Dr. Bruner points out that the crucial next phase is the emergence of the infant's pointing. With this behavior infants begin to direct the attention of people around them and to check to see whether the people have understood. Infants will point, then look back and forth between the caregiver's face and the object to see whether the caregiver is looking at the object (that is, to see whether joint reference has been established). When caregivers look at the object to which a child points, they usually provide a label for the object. Also at this time the caregiver may say, "Where's the _____?" Then the child will point to the object. This is usually followed by the caregiver's approval, often in the form of simple confirmation (for example, "That's right; there's the _____!"). Thus, the emergence of pointing coincides with the first signs of word comprehension.

Giving, showing, and especially pointing are the first conventional forms of communication. Prior to this time, infants and caregivers may have used a number of signals that they both understood, but anyone around children can understand what the children mean when they point. However, pointing is not yet symbolic (like words and some other gestures, which are described later in this section).

Early Vocal Play

As Dr. Sachs noted, six-month-old infants produce sounds in a pattern called babbling. Between six and seven months of age, babbling begins to change. A brief stage called vocal play occurs when children begin to experiment with long strings of syllable repetition. At this stage infants produce several sounds in one breath, and the infants begin to listen to others talking. Caregivers may hear things like "bababababa" and "dadada-dada" or even "babadadabada." If the caregiver responds to the child's sounds with a simple comment ("Yes, that's a nice doggie" or "Mmm, it feels good to have a dry diaper") or an imitation of the child's sounds, the infant is likely to repeat the sounds. However, the infant still does not connect the sound with meaning. Producing strings of sounds appears to be done simply because it is interesting and fun to do so—and it is even more interesting if the trusted caregiver joins in and a turn-taking game spontaneously develops.

Onset of Intentional Communication—Eight to Twelve Months

Between eight and twelve months of age, infants change from using generalized signals (crying, whining, cooing, laughing) in an automatic, reflexive way to understanding that their signals have a clear and definite effect on others, and the infants begin to use conventional symbols to communicate their desires. The symbols include gestures (for example, opening and closing the hand to gesture "give me" or "I want"), vocalizations (for example, "ahahah" to accompany the "give me" gesture), and, finally, words.

Most infants about eight or nine months old begin to interact with caregivers with the goal of communicating something. This is one of the most important transitions in infancy: the onset of intentional communication. From now until the end of this developmental period, there will be continuous refinement in the child's attempts to communicate. An expert on communication in infancy, Elizabeth Bates, notes that the critical change is that children at this stage understand that their signals will have an effect on their listener and know what the effect will be (Bates and others 1979, 1988). Thus, infants become deliberate givers of signals about the things they need or want; they become more equal partners in the vital game of communication.

However, the conversational turns children take at this stage will not necessarily include words. Early communications are expressed primarily through gestures, which are present in three substages of the development of communication (Bates and others 1979). In the earliest substage, infants use conventional rituals to interact with caregivers and other adults. The infants seem to take great delight in showing off for attention. They will play peek-a-boo, wave good-bye, give kisses, and shake the head for no. Infants also use a lot of jargon (that is, long strings of unintelligible sounds with adult intonation patterns). The tone of voice makes the jargon sound like questions, commands, or statements, even though the infants do not utter understandable words. Before long, the infants interact with the caregiver by showing an object, but they are not willing to release it, even though the original intention appeared to be to give or share.

Finally, the infants go beyond simply showing to giving and pointing. In doing so they appear to be commenting on the object of interest or requesting that it be given to them. These gestures, postures, actions, and vocalizations (for example, "ahahah") are forms by which infants communicate what they will soon be able to say with words. For example, reaching with an opening and closing hand and saying "ahahah" to ask for a cookie will soon be replaced by pointing and an utterance, such as "wandat" or "cookie." This is clearly an important step for the infant, a quantum leap in the ability to have an effect on the environment.

The attempts by the infant at intentional communication should be recognized and reinforced. Dr. Bates and others (1979) note three clear signs of the presence of intentionality in infants:

1. The child begins to look back and forth between the goal and the caregiver while emitting the signal (which may be a sound or a gesture). This action occurs in the earliest attempts at intentional communication, when the child is unsure of the new skill. Once the child is confident that the caregiver is attending to the signal, the child's looking back and forth decreases in frequency and is repeated only when the caregiver fails to respond.

2. The child changes the signal, depending on the caregiver's response. The child expands, adds, and substitutes signals until the goal has been reached or clearly will not

be reached. For example, on seeing an interesting object, the child may extend an arm toward it while opening and shutting the hand. If the caregiver does not give the object to him or her, the child may look back and forth between the object and the caregiver, say "eheheh," and continue to open and shut the extended hand. If that signal fails, the child may say "eheheh" louder and lean toward the object.

3. The form of the signals gradually changes toward abbreviated or exaggerated patterns that are appropriate only for communicating. For example, what begins as a reach and grasp is shortened to a quick open-and-shut movement of the hand, with the arm only partially extended. Because the child has had many experiences by this time with reaching and grasping in order to get objects, the purpose of the new abbreviated form may be only to enlist the caregiver's help. Similarly, grunts and fussing become ritualized into shorter, more regular sounds that shift in volume, depending on the caregiver's reaction (like the previous "eheheh" example). This latter development also suggests that the child recognizes the conventional aspect of communication. (*Conventional,* here, refers to the sounds or gestures whose functions are agreed on and recognized by both caregiver and child.) The sounds and gestures that become conventional are byproducts of the child's emerging use of signals to communicate.

The new experience of being able to communicate intentions successfully is a powerful motive for the child to acquire language skills (Moerk 1977, 49). It is important that caregivers recognize these attempts to communicate and use them as opportunities to further language and communication development by providing the appropriate labels, either in confirmation of the "comment" made by the child or in compliance with the child's "request."

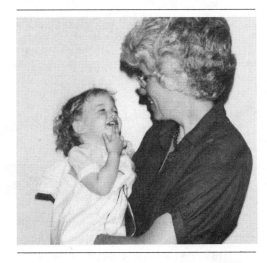

Earlier in this section, a give-and-take, turn-taking aspect to adult–infant interaction from the very early stages was discussed. Many developmental psychologists (including Daniel Stern, Jerome Bruner, and Elizabeth Bates) believe that this give-and-take lays the critical foundation for participating in conversation. By viewing all attempts at communication this way, a caregiver can stimulate language development even when the child has no words. The key is to treat all gestures and vocalizations as conversational turns. For example:

Child: (Gives toy dog to caregiver)
Caregiver: "Thank you! What a nice doggie." (Pets the dog)
Child: (Reaches for the dog) "Ahahah."
Caregiver: (Hands dog to child) "Here you are! Want to pet her?"

There is no harm in responding to the words the child has made up, although they are not words we use in adult language. For example, if a child calls the blanket "lala," give it to the child when he or she says "lala" and respond, "Here's your blanket."

Invented words are typical of children at this age and are an important sign that the children are developing as communicators. The children will later replace such words with words from the adult language. When children are this age, you want to show them that you understand them, and you want to communicate with them in a positive way; do not require that children use the adult word.

Use of Conventional Symbols— Twelve to Sixteen Months

During this period, children perfect their ability to get caregivers to pay attention to them and the topics that interest them. Intentional communication is well established. The children have made the important shift to the use of conventional symbols for communication. In the early stages, these symbols will be gestures as well as words.

About twelve months of age, children utter their first true words. These are likely to be words such as "mama," "dada," "papa," "da" (for dog), and "ba" (for bottle or baby). But the words may well be more idiosyncratic; for example, "ah" (hot) for cup or "moo" (moon) for outside. Usually, the words are used in the presence of the objects they represent, such as favorite toys, family members, or pets.

At the same time that first words appear, children begin to use a special class of gestures. The gestures (like first words) are made in the presence of particular objects but do not seem to be attempts to use the object for its real purpose. Examples include the child taking a toy cup and pretending to drink from it, holding a toy phone to the ear, taking a toy pillow from a doll crib and putting his or her head on it, or pretending to sleep. These gestures show that children understand the purpose or functional use of the objects and have come to classify them in a conventional way. Thus, the gestures may be considered a primitive form of naming an object or action and a categorization of the object or action as belonging to a particular conceptual class. For this reason the gestures are called *recognitory gestures* (Bates and others 1979, 1988). The conceptual skills needed to use recognitory gestures are the same skills needed to use words. The skills are simply being demonstrated in a gestural modality instead of the vocal modality.

There is one major difference between the gestures and words, however. Children generally use recognitory gestures to identify things for themselves, rarely to communicate with others. But the gestures are still important. In the same way that you follow the children's direction of gaze and name the object at which they have looked, you should apply a name to the object or activity represented by the gestures children produce. For example:

Child: (Picks up toy telephone and puts it to the ear)
Caregiver: "Oh, you've got the phone. Are you going to talk on the phone?"

There is one other class of gestures that you may see. These gestures are made far less frequently than recognitory gestures but are probably closer to a real word. These are empty-handed gestures carried out in the absence of an object (for example, making a turning movement with the hand to indicate turning a doorknob as a request to go outside). These gestures, too, should be responded to as though they were words. Indeed, all the gestures described in this section should be treated as though they were part of a conversational turn. You should never discourage children from using them.

By twelve months of age, most children recognize their own name when it is spoken. They can also follow simple instructions, especially when accompanied by a visual cue (for example, "say bye-bye" accompanied by a wave). Children understand the word *no* and the *no*

intonation and usually respond appropriately. Many children speak one or more words, although it is not uncommon for first words to occur as late as fifteen or

sixteen months of age. Words, jargon, and babble all occur together. During the next year of life, children's words increase, and jargon and babbling disappear. (This further development of language is discussed in the next section.)

Although children twelve to sixteen months old may produce only a few words, the children usually understand more than they can say. It is not unusual for them to understand between 60 and 150 words. (These estimates are based on norms gathered in San Diego, California, by Elizabeth Bates, Larry Fenson, and me.) *When* children begin to use words and *how* children produce words when they do start vary considerably. Some children retain sentencelike jargon mixed with words for quite a time; other children at this age begin to use single words, pronounced quite clearly. This variability reflects normal individual differences and is nothing to be concerned about.

Suggestions to Support Language Development

First, talk with the baby. For instance, say "hi" when you approach the infant and "bye" when you leave. Talk while you are bathing, diapering, and feeding the child. All these situations provide lots of opportunities to establish and maintain joint reference; to allow the child to communicate with you with gestures, vocalizations, and words; and to provide the names for the objects and activities in the child's daily life.

Use "caregiver talk" (also called baby talk or motherese) when you talk with infants. As Jacqueline Sachs pointed out in the previous section, this way of talking helps maximize children's skills when children are very young. Caregiver talk consists of simple but grammatically correct sentences. The pitch of the voice is higher than when you talk to adults, and intonation patterns (the up-and-down pitch changes of the voice) are more exaggerated. In caregiver talk you also use more repetition of words than you use in speech to adults.

Second, use the child's ability to participate in joint reference to teach him or her about the things in the world around the child. Observe the child carefully so you can use a child's focus of

attention as much as possible; that is, try to provide labels for or comment on things that the child is looking at, pointing to, and showing you rather than try to direct his or her attention. When you notice a child has followed your line of sight, it is also appropriate to label what you are looking at.

Use communicative modes, contexts, and intentions that are within the child's current competencies. Communicative modes used by children in this stage include gestures, sounds, body postures (for example, leaning forward in excitement), and words, usually produced within the context of gamelike rituals or daily activities. A child's intention is usually to get the adult to pay attention to some object of interest or to do something for the child. Another way to set up contexts for joint reference that can be fun for both caregiver and child is to carry the child around on "word walks," pointing to and labeling objects of interest to the child.

Third, provide opportunities for turn taking, a critical part of language use. There are many ways to do this with children in a natural way during this stage. Everyday activities that demonstrate turn taking can and should be done nonlinguistically (for example, physical play), vocally (for example, sound games, imitation), and linguistically (for example, words). The activity must be done without dominating the exchange of conversation. It is critical to remember that your goal is talking *with* children (that is, taking turns with them) rather than talking *to* them. Turn-taking routines in which the caregiver keeps asking "What's that?" should be avoided because those routines provide dead-end avenues for the child. The only turn possible after such a question is the answer, and then the conversation is over.

Because infants and toddlers are new to participating in conversation, it is important that you provide sufficient opportunity for the children to take their turn. After you take a turn, wait for a response from the child with clear, visible anticipation. Respond once, then wait for the child to respond. Attend carefully to the child's behavior as a potential turn in the conversation; the child may be participating nonverbally. Treat all of the child's behavior as communicative, as a turn in a beginning conversation. To make sure that you leave time for the child's turns, pay close attention to the child. Do not just rattle on. Keep your statements simple. Wait for the child's response; do not be afraid of a few seconds of silence. Here is an example of attentive turn taking:

> Caregiver: "Look at the doggie."
> (Pause)
>
> Caregiver: "He's big, huh!"
> (Or if the child said "doggie")
> "Yes, a doggie!"
> (Pause)
>
> Caregiver: "What a big doggie."

Give-and-take games, such as peek-a-boo and pat-a-cake, which can be carried out with lots of little variations, are excellent teaching tools. The games impose roles, turn taking, joint attention, and sequential structure while you and the child are having a great time.

Fourth, read simple, short stories when the child is about twelve months old, and read only when the child is quiet and alert. Picture books with realistic photographs or simple, clear drawings of familiar objects are a good means of introducing the child to the abstract representation of real objects with which the child has had experience. Be careful to read only if the child is interested. Do not force a child to be quiet or sit still, and be careful to respond to the child as a real partner in the conversation about the book.

Fifth, when a child demonstrates ability at a given level, it may be appropriate to do what Jerome Bruner (1983) calls "upping the ante." In other words, you can encourage performance at that new level. For example, if the child knows the word *car* and asks for a toy car by reaching or making a sound, you can respond by saying, "What do you want?" and pause briefly to allow the child to respond. The child may then say "car."

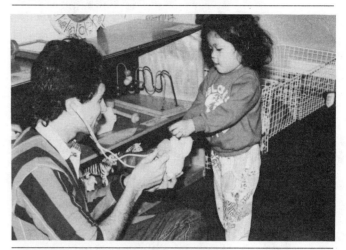

However, if the child does not say the word, you should not push the child to verbalize. Instead, the best approach is to name the item. For example, you may say, "Oh, you want the car." Pressuring the child to do or say something may discourage him or her from using language. In contrast, even when the child does not verbalize the "correct" word, your modeling of language encourages the child to participate in the next communicative interchange with you.

Warning Signs

All babies begin to babble when they are about six months old, including deaf babies. However, babbling will not continue beyond eight or nine months of age if the baby's hearing is not normal. If babbling stops, there is reason for concern. Dr. Sachs discusses this issue in detail in Section One of this guide and recommends important follow-up care if you suspect a hearing impairment.

Children are inquisitive beings who want to share new discoveries with their trusted caregivers. A problem may be indicated (1) if a child does not show an interest in making new discoveries by interacting with objects and caregivers in familiar environments; or (2) if the child does not engage in the typical, ritualized games of infancy, such as peek-a-boo and pat-a-cake.

By participating in joint reference activities, children gain some critical early experiences for language acquisition. Thus, other warning signs include (1) if a child at nine or ten months of age does not follow the direction of an adult's line of vision or pointing; or (2) if a child by eleven or twelve months of age does not give, show, and point to objects or does not engage in or initiate ritualized games with caregivers.

A child typically begins to use words when he or she is ten to fourteen months old. If a child does not use any words by the end of this period, the child should be watched carefully over the next few months to determine whether follow-up care is necessary.

References

Bates, Elizabeth, and others. *The Emergence of Symbols: Cognition and Communication in Infancy.* New York: Academic Press, Inc.,1979.

Bates, Elizabeth, and others. *From First Words to Grammar: Individual Differences and Dissociable Mechanisms.* New York: Cambridge University Press, 1988.

Bruner, Jerome. *Child's Talk: Learning to Use Language.* New York: W. W. Norton & Co., Inc., 1983.

Moerk, Ernst. *Pragmatic and Semantic Aspects of Early Language Development.* Baltimore: University Park Press, 1977.

Stern, Daniel. *The First Relationship: Infant and Mother.* Developing Child Series. Edited by Jerome Bruner and others. Cambridge, Mass.: Harvard University Press, 1977.

Stern, Daniel. *The Interpersonal World of the Infant: A View from Psychoanalysis and Developmental Psychology.* New York: Basic Books, Inc., 1985.

Developmental Milestones

The following developmental milestones are approximations at best. It is important to remember that there are great individual differences among children and that early language mastery is not necessarily associated with later language mastery. These milestones come from *Developmentally Appropriate Practice in Early Childhood Programs Serving Children from Birth Through Age 8.*

The infant:

- Understands many more words than can say. Looks toward two or more objects when named.
- Creates long babbled sentences.
- Shakes head no. Says two or three clear words.
- Looks at picture books with interest, points to objects.
- Uses vocal signals other than crying to gain assistance.
- Begins to use *me, you, I.*

Points to Consider

1. Do you pay attention to what infants are watching and comment on their interest? This is called establishing joint reference for conversation; it is important for you to respond to infants' interests and initiate conversation with the children.
2. When children point to an object or a person, do you respond by introducing words for what the children are looking at or playing with at that moment?
3. Do you pay close attention to children's glances and signs of interest so that you can interpret the environment for the children; that is, describe events, reassure the children with words and gestures, and so forth?

Caregiver's Practices

The caregiver working with mobile infants (six to sixteen months) can support language development and communication by:

1. Listening and talking with children
    The caregiver:

    - Uses caregiver or baby talk with infants; this consists of simple but grammatically correct sentences spoken in a generally higher pitch and pitch range than normally is used when talking with adults.
    - Talks with the baby, saying the same thing in the same situation (such as "hi" when coming close and "bye" when leaving).
    - Observes carefully the child's focus of attention and provides labels for or comments about things the child is looking at, pointing to, and showing rather than always tries to direct the child's attention.
    - Talks with the infant when feeding, diapering, and bathing the infant and uses the situations to discuss what is happening, engaging the baby in the routine activity itself, not distracting the baby from what is going on at the moment.
    - Responds to the infant's gestures, sounds, body postures, and facial expressions as forms of communication by also using gestures, sounds, body postures, and facial expressions.
    - Responds enthusiastically and with acceptance to the infant's first words, being careful not to correct the infant's first attempts at making words.
    - Uses gestures to demonstrate the meaning of words.
    - Elaborates on children's short phrases to help the children express their intended meaning.

2. Providing appropriate activities
    The caregiver:

    - Names and talks about infants' feelings, behaviors, activities, clothing, body parts, and so forth to help infants expand their vocabularies.
    - Takes "word walks": carries the child around the room, pointing to and naming objects of interest to the baby.
    - Uses turn-taking games in which the conversation continues (for example, sharing an object back and forth, making sure to wait for the infant to respond and take his or her turn).
    - Plays give-and-take games like peek-a-boo and pat-a-cake, using lots of little variations.
    - Reads simple, short stories when the baby is quiet and alert.

3. Communicating with parents
    The caregiver:

    - Has regular conversations with each infant's parents about new words, games, and other language activities the baby enjoys. In this way, both during caregiving at home and in the child care setting, parents and caregivers can support the infant's language development by using shared information about current developmental accomplishments.

Suggested Resources

Books and Articles

Bruner, Jerome. *Child's Talk: Learning to Use Language.* New York: W. W. Norton & Co., Inc., 1983.

A scholarly conceptual work appropriate for the serious student of early language development and communication. Focuses on the social aspects of language and the importance of the infant and mother establishing joint interaction. Discusses how negotiation is the foundation for communication in the young child.

DeVilliers, Peter, and Jill DeVilliers. *Early Language.* Developing Child Series. Cambridge, Mass.: Harvard University Press, 1979.

Written especially for the person who is not an academic or clinical linguist. Avoids technical jargon and conveys the complexity of language development in understandable terms. Complete and comprehensive in the discussion of early language; an excellent follow-up to this section of the guide.

Stern, Daniel. *The First Relationship: Infant and Mother.* Developing Child Series. Edited by Jerome Bruner and others. Cambridge, Mass.: Harvard University Press, 1977.

Considers in detail the importance of the first relationship and the infant's development. Focusing on the first six months of the relationship, this readable book provides detailed information about the topics outlined and discussed by Jacqueline Sachs and Donna Thal.

Thoman, Evelyn B., and Sue Browder. *Born Dancing: How Intuitive Parents Understand Their Baby's Unspoken Language and Natural Rhythms.* New York: Harper & Row Pubs., Inc., 1988.

Discusses in a very readable way the interaction and interrelationship between parent and child. For parents and caregivers alike, this book provides a sound child development basis for natural "dancing" with an infant. Different from most parenting books, this one is very supportive and refreshing in its approach.

Zero to Three, Vol. XI, No. 1 (September, 1990), 1–26.

Presents a series of articles on the communicative competence of infants and toddlers by writers such as Barry Prizant and Amy Wetherby, Lee McLean, Stanley Greenspan, and Diane Fraser. Topics range from the assessment of communication to intervention approaches with children who have language delays or language disorders.

Audiovisuals

Baby Talk. 1984. Videocassette, color, 49 minutes. Available from Media Guild, 11722 Sorrento Valley Road, Suite E, San Diego, CA 92121; telephone (619) 755-9191.

Examines modern research on child language development from fetal and early infant responses to speech, the innate abilities of language in humans, and the relationship of cognition and language. The film includes interviews with Jerome Bruner, Noam Chomsky, Dan Slobin, Peter Eimas, Catherine Snow, Jean Berko Gleason, Andrew Malzoff, and Eve Clark, all prominent American university linguists.

Out of the Mouths of Babes. Nature of Things Series, CBS Film K, 1973. Videocassette or 16mm film, color, 28 minutes. Available from Filmmakers Library, 124 E. 40th St., New York, NY 10016; telephone (212) 355-6545.

Provides an overview of chronological development of language in children from infancy to age six. Concentrating on the research of Peter and Jill DeVilliers from Harvard University, the film shows how children seem to learn a language on their own; the film notes the gradual progression from early babbling, gesturing, and one-word sentences to the use of complicated structures and linguistic concepts that extract rules of grammar from the language children hear around them.

Talking to Babies. Los Angeles: California State University, Los Angeles, Division of Special Education, 1989. Videocassette, color, 12 minutes. Available from Mother-Infant Communication Project, California State University, Los Angeles, Division of Special Education, 5151 University Drive, Los Angeles, CA 90032; telephone (213) 343-4414.

Demonstrates ways to talk with younger infants. Discusses the importance of responding to and supporting the infant's early communications.

The Program for infant toddler caregivers

Section Three: The Older Infant

Introduction

This section describes the language and communication of the older infant. Kathleen McCartney and Wendy Wagner Robeson provide a comprehensive discussion of the unfolding of language during this expansive toddler period. The authors also suggest how the caregiver can nurture this important period of communication for the young child.

Kathleen McCartney is Assistant Professor of Psychology at the University of New Hampshire. Previously, she was an Assistant Professor for five years at Harvard University. Dr. McCartney's research centers on the role of experience in language development. She has conducted studies on the effects of child care and early childhood intervention programs on the young child's language development.

Wendy Wagner Robeson, a doctoral student at Harvard Graduate School of Education at the time this book was being developed, is conducting research on the relationship between the mother's verbal feedback and the child's language development. Through the Boston area chapter of the National Association for the Education of Young Children, Ms. Robeson is involved in advocacy for better child care practices and what child care professionals can do to improve their working environment.

Emergence of Communication: Words, Grammar, and First Conversations

Kathleen McCartney and Wendy Wagner Robeson

The period from sixteen to thirty-six months of age marks many transitions in the young child's language and communication skills. At sixteen months of age, most children speak only one word at a time, although they may understand longer utterances addressed to them. By thirty-six months of age, most children are speaking complex sentences. This rapid transition seems to many parents and caregivers, and even to psycholinguists, like a miracle.

Overview of Language and Communication Issues

The ability to communicate involves many overlapping skills. Initially, the young child communicates through gestures, eye contact, and vocalizations. However, language offers the child greater flexibility in the messages that can be conveyed. In order to communicate, the young child must master the rules of both language and social interaction. The young child makes great progress toward mastering those rules from sixteen to thirty-six months of age and continues the process through the school years.

Children need to learn the four major rule-governed systems of language and communication, which are (1) phonology; (2) semantics; (3) syntax; and (4) pragmatics:

1. *Phonology* refers to sound patterns. The young child needs to acquire the rules by which sounds are combined in the language. Over time, the child's pronunciation of words will become more and more adultlike.

2. *Semantics* refers to the meaning of words. The young child needs to use agreed-on definitions. For example, a child might initially use the word *dog* to refer to all four-legged creatures. Through conversations and direct experiences, the child will eventually come to use this word, and others, as other people do.

3. *Syntax* refers to the grammatical rules by which words are combined. The system of grammatical rules for all languages is complex. When children begin to create two-word utterances, they use a primitive rule system. Over time, this system comes to match the adult rule system. Some rules are mastered easily. For example, in English, children quickly learn that the rule to make a past tense verb is usually to add *ed* to the verb.

4. *Pragmatics* refers to the social rules of language. The child needs to learn how to use language to accomplish goals. In other words the child needs to learn the various functions of language. For example, requests that are demands need to be made differently from requests that are polite inquiries.

How children acquire these rules is not clear. Certainly, language is learned through social experience. Yet children acquire certain skills with such great regularity that some researchers believe language is primarily a function of maturation (that is, language development occurs primarily from physiological growth rather than experience).

Stages of Language Communication

Children understand many words before they can say them. The term "productive language" refers to the language that children are able to say or produce on their own. The term "receptive language" refers to the language that children are able to understand or comprehend. The age at which an individual child will begin to use words varies greatly—some children begin at ten months, others at eighteen months of age.

One-word Stage

By sixteen months of age, most children are using language, one word at a time. The one-word stage is characterized by the following behaviors:

1. Babbling decreases, although it may continue until a child is about eighteen months old.
2. For some children, their first words are about things they can act on. The words may refer to objects or events that are familiar and important to the child (for example, family members).

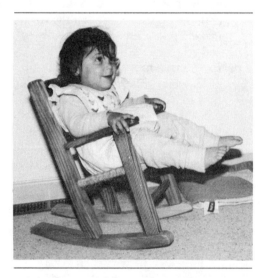

3. For some children, their first words may be shortened versions of phrases they have heard, such as "duhwanna" for "I don't want to."

These expressions often function as socially appropriate ways to communicate.

Children's vocabulary develops fast. By sixteen months of age, children may understand 50 to 150 words, but they may speak only 7 to 15 different words, on average. Later on, children will have vocabulary spurts, learn many more words, and use more words in their conversations. These spurts usually occur at the age of eighteen to twenty-four months and again at thirty to thirty-six months.

By the end of the one-word stage, a word may stand for a whole message. For example, a child might say "milk" to communicate "I want more milk." When a whole message is conveyed in one word, the word is called a "holophrase" (DeVilliers and DeVilliers 1978).

Two-word Stage

Children's transition to the two-word stage occurs gradually between the ages of eighteen and thirty months. Again, there is great variability among children on when this takes place. Children begin to string words together but do not include all the necessary grammatical parts in their utterances (Schickedanz and others 1983). This stage is referred to as "telegraphic speech."

A child's speech resembles a telegram; only the essential parts are included. Words that are left out include articles (for example, "the"), conjunctions (for example, "and"), prepositions (for example, "over"), and helping verbs (for example, "to be"). For instance, a child might say "put shoe foot" for "put the shoe on my foot" or "baby sleep" for "the baby is sleeping." Even so, the child's language is rule governed, although the rules are not as sophisticated as the adult rule system children eventually acquire.

The early two-word utterances are short and simple. At this stage, along with all the others, caregivers must make an effort to understand the child's intentions (Schickedanz and others 1983).

Multiword Stage (Sentences)

With time, children's sentences grow longer, become more varied and more complex, and contain more and more words. Between the ages of two and four years, children begin to form grammatically correct sentences, although their rule system is still not complete. As children's sentences become longer, they become syntactically more complex.

Children typically use consistent patterns that sound different from the way adults talk. For example, as they learn to ask questions, many children use sentences like "Where kitty is hiding?" or "Why the lady can't go?" Do not think of these sentence constructions as mistakes. They are really signs that children are working out the complex rules of the language.

By three years of age, the child's vocabulary consists of more than 300 words. This vocabulary explosion is accompanied by the growth in three-or-more-word utterances. The child at this stage has moderately complex speech and is more mature in thought and social interactions. Multiword utterances use more sophisticated language. The sentences involve more complex syntax and more semantic knowledge. The child can talk of the past, present, and future and has learned how to use language to get things done. However, there are still differences between the child's language and the adult's. For example, children may overuse a word (calling all four-legged animals "dogs") or underuse a word (using "dog" to refer only to one specific dog).

Caregiver Talk

When adults speak to young children, they speak in a different manner from that used when they speak to another adult. They adapt their language so it is easier to understand. These speech adjustments, which seem to occur automatically to help adults talk with young children, are made by adults speaking almost every language. This conversational style used with children has been referred to as "baby talk," "motherese," or, more precisely, "child-directed speech."

Child-directed Speech

Child-directed speech can be identified by eight key features (Snow 1986). The adult using child-directed speech:

1. Speaks with clear pronunciation
2. Speaks at a slower rate
3. Speaks in shorter sentences
4. Repeats the same utterance two or more times
5. Speaks in a higher than normal pitch
6. Uses simple words
7. Speaks with exaggerated intonation so that the speech has a singsong quality
8. Speaks in grammatically simple sentences

There is some debate about the functions of child-directed speech. Some researchers believe its function is merely to signal to the child that communicating will be easier to "practice" now. Other researchers believe that adults continuously fine-tune the complexity of their language to a child's level of understanding. This debate mostly concerns the child's development of syntax. There seems to be little debate over whether children profit from meaningful language exchanges with the adults in their lives.

In one child care study, children whose caregivers engaged them in verbal interaction scored higher on four measures of language and communication. Verbal interaction among peers was not positively associated with language development. Although peers serve an important social function, the verbal environment peers provide cannot replace that of more experienced communicators, such as caregivers and parents (McCartney 1984).

Caregiver Strategies

Caregivers can use a number of strategies to promote language development and communication. To test your skill in promoting language skills, ask yourself the following questions (see Mattick 1981). The answer to every question should be yes.

1. Am I involved in a back-and-forth interaction?

   Sometimes adults engage in monologues rather than in real communication. As a caregiver you should encourage the child to engage in conversations. It is also important to check who is doing the most talking—the child or you.

2. Am I really listening to what the child is saying?

   You should not interrupt the child as soon as you think you know what has been said. By really listening, you can ask the child for more details and give the child alternatives to consider.

3. Do I finish my sentences and thereby my thoughts?

   If you want to be understood by the child and want to be a good language model, you should try not to leave the child hanging during conversations.

4. Do I avoid using the same phrase in my interactions with the child, such as "That's nice"?

   The use of pat answers does nothing to promote verbal interaction between the child and you. Using a variety of expressions causes children to think.

5. Do I provide activities that encourage verbal interactions?

   Children should be engaged in activities that naturally lead to verbal interaction with both you and other children. Such activities include story time, picture discussions, and informal conversations.

6. Do I initiate one-to-one conversations with individual children concerning everyday events?

   It is important to have individual conversations with children. They can talk about events that are happening in their lives and that are

presently taking place. These conversations show children that you think they are worth listening to. Also, the one-to-one conversations give shy children a chance to talk.

7. Do I make an effort to understand what a child is trying to say?

   You may really have to try to understand some children because their pronunciation is unclear or because they are still at the one- or two-word stage. You need to make the effort because children will begin to acquire communicative competence if they are able to get the message of their utterances across to you.

8. Do I allow a child to finish a sentence?

   Although you may be tempted to finish children's sentences for them, it is important that you not do so. Children need to figure out how to communicate their messages effectively. This will never happen if someone else always completes their sentences.

9. Do I promote self-confidence in the child as a communicator?

   When you actively listen to the child, let the child finish what is being said, and try to understand what the child is saying; then you are promoting self-confidence in the child as a communicator. With self-confidence the child will be willing to risk other attempts at communication. Remember that communication occurs through rich interaction between children and adults.

10. Do I model grammatically correct language?

    You need to remember that as caregiver you serve as a language model for children. Therefore, you should try to use grammatically correct language.

11. Do I expand and extend the child's language?

    You should listen to the child and try to expand the child's language and extend the topic that the child raised in the conversation. When you expand the child's language, you repeat what the child has said but make it grammatically correct. When you *extend* a topic, you partially repeat what the child has said but also add more information.

When to Encourage Language and Communication

A sensitive caregiver who pays close attention to an individual child will know

from the child's behavior when he or she is ready, interested, and motivated to engage in language activities and conversation. When the child is ready, nearly every exchange can be used to encourage language and communication. Some situations seem to lend themselves particularly well to language interaction (Maxim 1980). These activities can involve the caregiver with one or more children.

Story Time

Children enjoy stories, either told or read aloud. At first it is important that the stories are about things with which the children are familiar. Short books with simple concepts and clear pictures are best at this stage. As children develop, they will also enjoy stories about make-believe, humor, new places, and exotic animals. Stories are valuable because they (1) expose children to rich and varied language; (2) help children discover new words, meanings, and understandings; and (3) promote imaginative thought.

Picture Discussions

A picture file can consist of large, colorful, uncomplicated pictures that stimulate verbal exchanges. The pictures can come from magazines, old calendars, advertisements, and discarded books and should be clear and free from confusing details. The pictures should be attached to construction paper or tagboard. An especially good way to protect pictures is to laminate them or cover them with clear, adhesive plastic. These pictures can be posted in the room at the child's eye level, used to make a picture book, or used as an "activity" by the children to talk about what they see and what they think about the picture.

Picture discussions are valuable because they (1) motivate children to discuss what they see; and (2) inspire children to make up stories. Caregivers must form their questions in a way that moves children from stating what they see to discussing the picture at higher levels of interpretation. Children can also make up stories from a series of pictures.

Make-believe and Fantasy Play

Toddlers love make-believe and fantasy play. An activity area that includes a variety of simple dress-up materials and other thematic props (for example, a toy camera or cooking utensils) sets the stage for children's fantasy play. Having puppets available also encourages children to use language through pretend play. Puppets can be used in caregiver-initiated activities in one-to-one or small-group situations.

Informal Conversations

Children should be encouraged to speak freely both to the caregiver and to other children. The caregiver provides verbal stimulation to help children associate language with their experiences. These conversations might occur during mealtimes, in the dramatic play area, or by the swings.

Warning Signs

As we have stressed, there is great variation in the age at which children begin to talk and the rate at which language development proceeds. However, caregivers may need to refer parents to appropriate professionals if children stand out noticeably from their age group in relation to language development, especially if the delay or deviance in language seems to be causing problems with the children's intellectual or social development. The reasons for language delay include:

1. Physical or structural deficits (for example, hearing loss)
2. Physiological or neurological impairments (for example, cerebral palsy)
3. Mental retardation
4. Emotional problems (Dumtschin 1988)

Children with delayed language development have limited vocabularies and less variation in their sentence structure than do other children their age. They may make more grammatical errors and have difficulty combining different kinds of information in single sentences. These children may have problems talking about the future. They may misunderstand questions and often are misunderstood. The children may play more by themselves because they show fewer social forms of play. They may use short, simple sentences and have difficulty maintaining a conversation (Dumtschin 1988).

It is important to detect early language delays and provide intervention because language is so important for the child's continuing development. Five percent of all school-age children show delayed or deviant language (88 percent of these children have problems with articulation or stuttering) (DeVilliers and DeVilliers 1978). Language delays are a common source of children's educational difficulty during the school years. Poor language ability can also lead to poor social skills (White 1987). Delayed language may involve receptive or expressive language skills or both (Reich 1986).

Caregivers are not speech/language pathologists; they cannot diagnose prob-

lems or decide on appropriate therapy. However, if at any age, especially by three years of age, a child does not seem to be developing language normally, the caregiver may suggest to the child's parents that they consult a language specialist (Genishi and Dyson 1987). The National Association for Hearing and Speech Action (NAHSA) is a helpful resource for locating a speech/language pathologist nearby. Call 1-800-638-8255 for a referral. Another association that can provide more information related to language problems in young children is the American Speech-Language-Hearing Association, 10801 Rockville Pike, Rockville, MD 20852.

References

Bzoch, K. R., and R. League. *The Bzoch-League Receptive-Expressive Emergent Language Scale*. Baltimore, Md.: University Park Press, Inc., 1970.

DeVilliers, Jill G., and Peter A. DeVilliers. *Language Acquisition.* Cambridge, Mass.: Harvard University Press, 1978.

Dumtschin, J. U. "Recognize Language Development and Delay in Early Childhood," *Young Children,* Vol. 43 (1988), 16–24.

Genishi, Celia, and Anne H. Dyson. *Language Assessment in the Early Years.* Language and Learning for Human Service Professions, Vol. 4. Edited by Cynthia Wallat and Judith Green. Norwood, N.J.: Ablex Publishing Corp., 1987.

Hetherington, E. M., and Ross D. Parke. *Child Psychology: A Contemporary Viewpoint.* New York: McGraw-Hill Publishing Co., 1979.

Mattick, I. "The Teacher's Role in Helping Young Children Develop Language Competence," in *Language in Early Childhood Education* (Revised edition). Edited by Courtney B. Cazden. Washington, D.C.: National Association for the Education of Young Children, 1981, pp. 107–125.

Maxim, George W. *The Very Young: Guiding Children from Infancy Through the Early Years.* Belmont, Calif.: Wadsworth Publishing Co., 1980.

McCartney, K. "The Effect of Quality of Day Care Environment Upon Children's Language Development," *Developmental Psychology,* Vol. 20 (1984), 244–260.

Reich, P. A. *Language Development.* Englewood Cliffs, N.J.: Prentice Hall, 1986.

Schickedanz, Judith A., and others. *Strategies for Teaching Young Children* (Second edition). Englewood Cliffs, N.J.: Prentice Hall, 1983.

Snow, C. E. "Conversations with Children," in *Language Acquisition: Studies in First Language Development* (Second edition). Edited by Paul Fletcher and Michael Garman. New York: Cambridge University Press, 1986, pp. 69–89.

White, Burton L. *Educating the Infant and Toddler.* Lexington, Mass.: Lexington Books, 1987.

Developmental Milestones

The following developmental milestones are approximations at best. It is important to remember that there are great individual differences among children and that early language mastery is not necessarily associated with later language mastery. These milestones come from several sources (Bzoch and League 1970; Hetherington and Parke 1979; Maxim 1980; and White 1987).

Fourteen to Sixteen Months

Receptive skills (what the child can understand):
1. Can respond to a verbal request to get or do something
2. Recognizes named objects
3. Recognizes named body parts
4. Understands approximately 50 words

Expressive skills (what the child can say):
1. Can speak 7 to 15 words
2. Speaks by using words and gestures

Sixteen to Eighteen Months

Receptive skills:
1. Understands straightforward questions
2. Can group words into categories
3. Understands approximately 100 words

Expressive skills:
1. Begins to use more words than gestures when speaking
2. Begins to repeat overheard words
3. Speaks between 20 and 25 words

Eighteen to Twenty Months

Receptive skills:
1. Can point to body parts when asked
2. Can respond to commands
3. Can respond to personal pronouns (me, her, him)

Expressive skills:
1. Speaks at least 25 words

Twenty to Twenty-two Months

Receptive skills:
1. Can follow two or three commands in a row
2. Recognizes many named objects

Expressive skills:
1. Begins speaking in two-word utterances
2. Speaks many new words

Twenty-two to Twenty-four Months

Receptive skills:
1. Listens for the meaning of what is heard
2. Can understand complex (compound) sentences

Expressive skills:
1. Seems to create his or her own phrases
2. Begins speaking in three-word utterances
3. Begins using pronouns

Twenty-four to Twenty-seven Months

Receptive skills:
1. Recognizes less familiar body parts
2. Recognizes family member category names (father, mother, grandfather)
3. Understands more than 300 words

Expressive skills:
1. Speaks in two- or three-word utterances
2. Uses pronouns correctly
3. Speaks between 200 and 275 words

Twenty-seven to Thirty Months

Receptive skills:
1. Understands relationships between objects and their functions
2. Understands size
3. May understand up to 750 words

Expressive skills:
1. Can name at least one color
2. Uses pronoun when refers to self
3. Speaks in three- to five-word sentences
4. Has mastered the vowel sounds and many of the consonant sounds, although still has problems with articulation
5. May speak between 400 and 450 words

Thirty to Thirty-three Months

Receptive skills:
1. Understands common verbs
2. Understands common adjectives
3. Understands complex sentences

Expressive skills:
1. Names own gender
2. Can say own first and last names
3. Can talk about own drawings

Thirty-three to Thirty-six Months

Receptive skills:
1. Demonstrates understanding of "how" and "why" questions
2. Understands prepositions (in, out)
3. Can follow three commands given at once
4. Understands more than 1,000 words

Expressive skills:
1. Can talk of the past
2. Uses some plurals of nouns
3. Uses utterances of somewhat similar grammatical complexity to those of an adult
4. May speak between 800 and 900 words

Points to Consider

1. Am I careful to listen to what children are saying? Do I wait my turn to talk, allowing children to finish their thoughts and sentences?
2. Do I finish my sentences so children can understand what I am trying to say?
3. Am I on "automatic pilot" when I verbally respond to children, or am I really conscious and present at the moment so I can respond appropriately to children's unique inquiries?
4. Do I model grammatically correct language while making my language simple enough for children to understand?
5. Do I support children's feelings of competence and self-esteem in my conversations with children?

Caregiver's Practices

The caregiver working with older infants and toddlers (sixteen to thirty-six months) can support language development and communication by:

1. Listening and talking with children
   The caregiver:
   • Uses everyday conversations with children to enrich and expand their vocabulary.

- Helps children learn, understand, and use words to express thoughts, ideas, questions, feelings, and physical needs.
- Is sensitive to children's natural humor; observes whether something seems funny to children and laughs with, not at, them.

2. Providing appropriate activities
   The caregiver:
   - Provides opportunities for children to represent their ideas nonverbally through activities such as painting, making music, and moving creatively.
   - Writes down toddlers' stories and labels their drawings, showing the relationship between spoken and printed words.
   - Looks at picture books with children, has a special story time, and engages children, individually and in groups of two or three, in a variety of activities that encourage both listening and talking.
   - Supports children's interest in make-believe and fantasy play by providing materials such as dress-up clothes, props, and puppets.

3. Communicating with parents
   The caregiver:
   - Discusses with parents the importance of back-and-forth communication between the toddler and the adult and the importance of individual conversations with the child—involving only the child and the parent.
   - Points out that when adults listen carefully to what children say, children learn that they are competent communicators and can get their needs met by talking.
   - Points out that by listening carefully to what children are

saying and by asking for more details and suggesting alternatives, parents can encourage more communication. Parents can also support their children by hearing what they say and responding to their inquiries.
   - Shares with parents the importance of the parents modeling for their child grammatically correct language and completed sentences, thereby completed thoughts, so the child can understand the parent.

Suggested Resources

Books and Articles

The following NAEYC publications are available from the National Association for the Education of Young Children, 1834 Connecticut Ave., N.W., Washington, DC 20009-5786.

Jalongo, Mary R. *Young Children and Picture Books: Literature from Infancy to Six.* NAEYC Publication #160.

Describes what constitutes high-quality literature and art for children's books. Explains how good books benefit young children's development.

Language in Early Childhood Education (Revised edition). Edited by Courtney B. Cazden. NAEYC Publication #131.

Gives a clear, straightforward description of language development and how it affects work with young children.

Schickedanz, Judith A. "Helping Children Learn About Reading." NAEYC Publication #520 (brochure).

Gives the reader a brief look at how to make learning to read a meaningful part of children's lives.

Schickedanz, Judith A. *More Than the ABCs: The Early Stages of Reading and Writing.* NAEYC Publication #204.

Offers clear suggestions about how to organize your home or classroom without work sheets or drill so children can experience reading and writing as a joyous and meaningful part of life. Provides practical advice based on how children really learn to read.

Thoman, Evelyn B., and Sue Browder. *Born Dancing: How Intuitive Parents Understand Their Baby's Unspoken Language and Natural Rhythms.* New York: Harper & Row Pubs., Inc., 1988.

Discusses in a very readable way the interaction and interrelationship between parent and child. For parents and caregivers alike, this book provides a sound child development basis for natural "dancing" with an infant. Different from most parenting books, this one is very supportive and refreshing in its approach.

Zero to Three, Vol. XI, No.1 (September, 1990), 1–26.

Presents a series of articles on the communicative competence of infants and toddlers by writers such as Barry Prizant and Amy Wetherby, Lee McLean, Stanley Greenspan, and Diane Fraser. Topics range from the assessment of communication to intervention approaches with children who have language delays or language disorders.

Audiovisuals

Baby Talk. 1984. Videocassette, color, 49 minutes. Available from Media Guild, 11722 Sorrento Valley Road, Suite E, San Diego, CA 92121; telephone (619) 755-9191.

Examines modern research on child language development from fetal and early infant responses to speech, the innate abilities of language in humans, and the relationship of cognition and language. The film includes interviews with Jerome Bruner, Noam Chomsky, Dan Slobin, Peter Eimas, Catherine Snow, Jean Berko Gleason, Andrew Malzoff, and Eve Clark, all prominent American university linguists.

McCarthy, J. *Reading and Young Children.* NAEYC Video Publication #808. Available from NAEYC, 1834 Connecticut Ave., NW, Washington, DC 20009-5786.

Describes what teachers and caregivers can say to parents who want their children to read in preschool. Makes an excellent companion for *More Than the ABCs* by Judith A. Schickedanz.

Out of the Mouths of Babes. Nature of Things Series, CBS Film K, 1973. Videocassette or 16mm film, color, 28 minutes. Available from Filmmakers Library, 124 E. 40th St., New York, NY 10016; telephone (212) 355-6545.

Provides an overview of chronological development of language in children from infancy to age six. Concentrating on the research of Peter and Jill DeVilliers from Harvard University, the film shows how children seem to learn a language on their own; the film notes the gradual progression from early babbling, gesturing, and one-word sentences to the use of complicated structures and linguistic concepts that extract rules of grammar from the language children hear around them.

Talking to Toddlers. Los Angeles: California State University, Los Angeles, Division of Special Education, 1989. Videocassette, color, 12 minutes. Available from Mother-Infant Communication Project, California State University, Los Angeles, Division of Special Education, 5151 State University Drive, Los Angeles, CA 90032; telephone (213) 343-4414.

Demonstrates ways to talk with toddlers as they begin to use words and then sentences. Discusses the importance of these early communications in supporting language development in the preschool years.

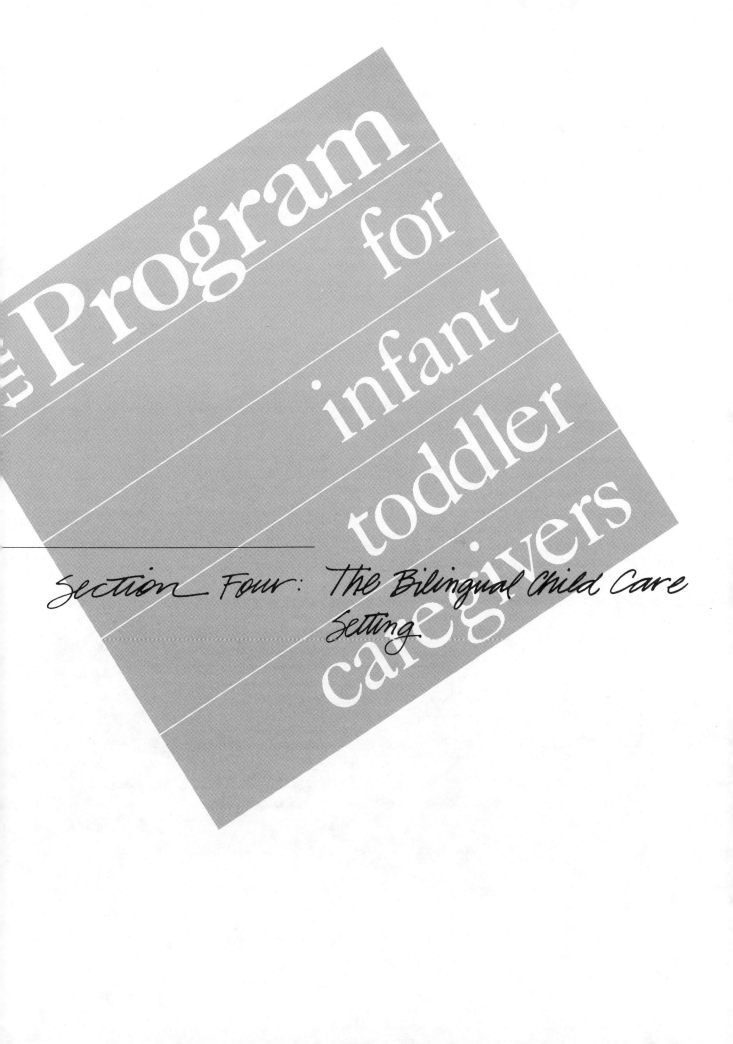

The Program for infant toddler caregivers

Section Four: The Bilingual Child Care Setting

Introduction

In this section Eugene E. Garcia explores and dispels some of the common but inaccurate myths about a child learning more than one language early in life. He also makes a strong point about supporting the child's home or native language during the very early development of the child's language and communication skills. In addition, Dr. Garcia discusses the importance of communicating frequently with parents about their child, using the native language of the family in both formal and informal communication. The implications for multilingual child care settings are also described.

Eugene E. Garcia is Dean of Social Sciences and Codirector of the National Center for Research on Cultural Diversity and Second Language Acquisition at the University of California at Santa Cruz where previously he was Professor of Education. He has served as a postdoctoral fellow in human development at Harvard University and as a National Research Council fellow; he was also the recipient of a three-year national Kellogg fellowship. Dr. Garcia is involved in various community activities and is a member of several boards of directors of local organizations. He has published extensively in the area of language teaching and bilingual development.

Caring for Infants in a Bilingual Child Care Setting

Eugene E. Garcia

Caring for young children is one of the most important activities in society. The early years of life build the foundation for all that follows. This is particularly true for the social communication skill we call language. Language provides a vital and complex social repertoire that allows young children to understand and influence their environment. Caregivers and infants establish an important social relationship that depends on the emerging communicative skills of the infant and the "expert" communicative ability of the caregiver.

The Importance of the Child's Home Language

First and foremost, infants and toddlers need a rich linguistic environment in order to thrive and develop their language and communication competence. The first three sections of this guide describe in detail the development of language for the child from birth to three years of age and the critical role of the caregiver in supporting and enhancing that development. When an infant or toddler is first learning language, caregivers should provide a rich linguistic environment, both at home and in the child care setting, that supports the native language and the culture of the infant's family. This is true regardless of the family's language or cultural group. When infants are cared for by the family, the native language and culture are supported automatically. However, when children are cared for outside the family, the native language of the caregiver(s) may or may not match that of the infant. For families whose home language is not English, the fact that English is the prevailing language in many child care settings in the United States raises some concerns and issues that need to be considered.

Preserving a family's home language and cultural heritage is very important to the identity and sense of well-being of the entire family. For young children, cultural and linguistic identity provides a strong and important sense of self and family belonging. This in turn supports a wide range of learning capabilities, not the least of which is learning a second language (Cummins 1979a, 1979b, 1981; Krashen 1981; Lambert 1972). Another important consideration is the relationship of language development and learning about one's culture. Language learning for the young child is closely tied to cultural learning. The specific issues of culture as they relate to language are discussed in Section Five of this guide.

Given the cultural and language diversity of infants and toddlers being cared for outside the family, how can caregivers best support and enrich each child's native language in a bilingual child care setting?

First, all child care programs need well-trained, sensitive caregivers who speak the same language as the child and represent the child's cultural group. Although this is not a current reality, it is a goal to strive for to support all children and families in the United States.

Second, and equally important, all caregivers need to become educated about and sensitive to the issues of language and culture, regardless of their own language background and cultural heritage. This understanding and sensitivity will support children, families, and providers as children grow and develop in a culturally diverse society.

Third, caregivers need to understand several important characteristics of early bilingual experience to provide the most effective care to children in nonnative language environments.

This section explores several important issues:

- Actions caregivers can take to ensure a supportive, responsive environment in which communication thrives
- Myths about the supposed negative effects of bilingualism
- Communication with the family and an understanding of the family's social circumstances

Providing a Supportive Language Learning Environment

The optimal situation for supporting native language learning is one in which the caregiver's language matches that of the infant and the infant's family. Providing the native language in the caregiving

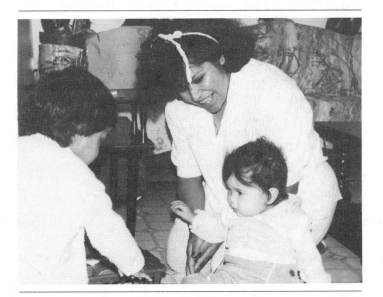

situation supports and reinforces the many rich encounters with language that the infant has within the family. As children begin speaking, it is very important that they be exposed to and use their native language in a wide variety of ways because language and intellectual development are closely related.

When young children hear their native language spoken in familial settings and in the wider community, they are exposed to more words, more complex grammar, and more complex ideas, thoughts, and concepts. This broad range of linguistic and cognitive experiences in natural situations enriches the development of both language and intellectual functioning in the older infant and preschool child (Heath 1986).

Infants develop and thrive linguistically in rich but natural communication interactions. They do not require any special teaching (Ervin-Tripp 1973). In other words, caregivers should not formally teach any language. What caregivers do naturally is what supports native language learning. We know that "caregivers intuitively modify their speech to young children in such a way as to make it more easily understood" (McLaughlin 1985, 60).

Jacqueline Sachs, in the first section of this guide, discusses why it is important and appropriate for caregivers to use baby talk with infants. We also know that infants are like sponges in the sense that they "receive" language and store up an incredible amount of language long before they "produce" spoken language. Activities such as telling stories, singing, rhyming, and chanting in the child's home language, along with generally talking with the baby, support language development and are enjoyable for children and caregivers. These activities "bathe" the infant in a rich linguistic environment. The nonverbal communication that accompanies spoken language is also very powerful and communicates an emotional context for the language experiences.

It is important for the caregiver who speaks the child's home language to communicate in a variety of ways, especially with the older infant and toddler. In one-to-one interactions with the young and mobile infant, the caregiver will speak intimately with the child, using informal language forms and simple, familiar words. As the infant gets older, the caregiver's communication about objects and activities in the environment and use of words and language forms will naturally become more diverse and varied. The caregiver will model yet another form and context for language when he or she speaks to the child's parents and other caregivers.

In all of these different conversations, the child receives exposure to language and communication in his or her native language. This exposure to vocabulary and grammar in a natural setting provides the child with a firm foundation in the native language. And this foundation enables the child to learn a second language more easily. The child's rich and varied involvement in his or her native language, before the child attempts to learn a second language, sets the stage for second language learning (Cummins 1981; Duncan and DeAvila 1979; Legarreta 1979).

But what if it is impossible to provide native-language or bilingual caregivers? Will not this harm the linguistic development of the infants? Certainly, if the caregiver refuses to interact with the infant by ignoring the child's natural communicative attempts, the infant will soon stop communicating. However, more than 60 percent of any communicative act is nonverbal. Infants communicate initially by pointing, crying, wiggling, nodding, grimacing, and so on. The best approach to handling a language mismatch in a caregiving situation is for the caregiver to attend to all the infant's communicative signals and to respond naturally with understanding and a visible willingness to communicate.

Regardless of the language environment, all infants attempt communication. Young children have not yet learned to be afraid of making mistakes; infants will "risk" communicating with caregivers regardless of the language the infants speak. Caregivers should do the same. The child will not be mixed up or confused by the use of an unfamiliar language by the caregiver as long as that communication is authentic.

Caregivers can help with the language mismatch by playing tapes of stories, rhymes, and songs in the child's native language. Toys, photos, pictures, and books that show the child's home culture will give the child things to point out, name, and talk about in his or her native language.

Still, it is important to find someone who can speak the infant's native language (a parent, relative, or community volunteer), even if that person cannot be the child's primary caregiver in the child care program. The infant must feel welcome in this nonhome environment. Hearing his or her language will assist greatly. However, caregivers whose native language is different from the child's should never fear that their language is "bad" for the child and should not hesitate to speak to the child just as they would to infants from their own language group. The language mismatch is simply not optimal for the child's overall language and cognitive development.

Dismissing Myths About Bilingualism

Current research shows that bilingualism is not harmful; young children are quite capable of learning more than one language. However, as discussed earlier, a firm foundation in the home language is recommended before the young child learns a second language. The very young child should be given every opportunity to learn his or her home language fully. This means that optimally, from birth to age four, children are cared for in settings that support their native or home language.

However, because many young children are exposed to a nonnative language when they are cared for outside their homes, it is important to dispel some commonly held myths about the effects of bilingualism. What does

bilingualism add or subtract in the arithmetic of language development? Is bilingualism bad? Does it lead to linguistic delays, communicative confusion, or other developmental risks? The early research on the effects of bilingualism painted a bleak picture. For instance, in 1952 one researcher concluded: "There can be no doubt that the child reared in a bilingual environment is handicapped in his language growth" (Thompson 1952, 162). In essence, this understanding of bilingualism concluded that learning one language is hard enough, so learning two must be at least twice as hard, particularly for the young child.

Present-day research has shown this conclusion to be false, a myth perpetuated by misunderstood "common sense." Throughout the world and in the United States, more up-to-date research has shown that young children who live in supportive and nurturing bilingual environments do not suffer linguistically

from those environments. This research has carefully documented the development of several types of bilingualism and compared the results to the development of English in monolingual children. Analysis of these comparisons clearly indicates that bilingual children, at both early and late periods of development, do not differ significantly from monolingual children on measures of vocabulary development, phonological development (comprehending and producing the sounds of a language), syntactic development (understanding and using grammatical rules), and the development of the many nuances of communication.

An interesting and quite important finding, sometimes negatively interpreted, is that bilingual children may move through a phase of language mixing. The children are sometimes observed to use two languages as if they were one. For example, a Spanish/English bilingual child may say "Yo quiero *play*" (I want to *play*) or "Yo estaba *playendo*" (I was *playing*). In such cases the child is using English vocabulary or grammar within a Spanish linguistic context. In the past, such instances of mixed language usage were interpreted as evidence of language confusion. Today we understand those mixed language instances as a normal developmental occurrence for some bilingual children. Mixed language usage is much like overgeneralization (saying "sheeps" for the plural "sheep" or "deers" for the plural "deer") in monolingual English-speaking children.

In the United States, millions of young children are exposed to two languages, particularly Spanish and English. However, there are more than 100 languages spoken in combination with English in this country's families. An article in *American Psychologist,* a highly respected professional journal, reaches the following conclusion about bilingual children:

The research evidence suggests that bilingual acquisition involves a process that builds on an underlying base for both languages. There does not appear to be a competition over mental processes by the two languages and there are even possible cognitive advantages to bilingualism. It is evident that the duality of the languages per se does not hamper the overall language proficiency or cognitive development of bilingual children. (Hakuta and Garcia 1989, 376)

Although bilingualism was once considered a "bad habit," best eliminated as soon as possible, today we can rest easy about the supposed harm bilingualism causes and instead appreciate and support the communicative development of the bilingual child. But if bilingualism is not harmful, should it be promoted? Should non-English-speaking infants hear as much English as possible? Should they receive early and consistent exposure to English so they can begin to acquire the English they will need to be successful in this country? Should child care providers attempt to teach English to non-English-speaking infants? Is an English-speaking care situation early in life exactly what is needed?

If the family's native language is not English, each of these questions can be answered with a clear no. We now know that the better a young child learns the native language and the many cognitive and social skills needed to communicate effectively in that language, the better the child will master the complexities of communicating in a second language.

Communicating with Families

Through exchanging information, parents can help caregivers provide an environment that supports native language learning in infants and toddlers. When the parents' native language is not English, they often prefer to exchange information with the child's caregiver in their native language. A number of

formal and informal activities and strategies can aid the communication between caregiver and family when the two have different native languages.

When information must be given to parents in a formal setting (for example, in a workshop on child care or when state regulations must be explained), it should be provided by a professional who speaks the parents' native language. All parents appreciate these kinds of information and education sessions. But parents will often understand the information only if it is presented in their native language.

Informal situations for interaction can be quite useful. Providing a "parents' corner," perhaps, with simple refreshments for parents when they drop off or pick up children allows for conversation in which caregivers and parents can chat about the day's happenings or community events. This kind of informal setting is much more tolerant of linguistic diversity. The informal interactions allow each participant, caregivers and parents alike, to learn and practice aspects of the language that is foreign to him or her. Parents always appreciate the caregiver's learning and using greetings and other simple phrases in their native language.

The family must be kept informed at all times of the relevant activities, moods, and health of their infant. To accomplish

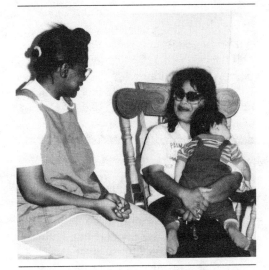

this, the caregiver and family must communicate in the family's native language. In some situations an older bilingual child can serve as a translator, although this may place the bilingual child in an awkward situation in which he or she cannot serve as an effective translator. Do not count on children's translations to inform the family. Always try to use bilingual adults if translators are necessary.

It may also be necessary to communicate with people other than the infant's parents, because many families count on older siblings, aunts, uncles, or grandparents to serve as primary caregivers. Any formal written communication, such as letters, forms, or newsletters, should be in the family's native language.

Infant caregivers may be perceived as members of the extended family. This role requires a much different communicative style from the one that is usually expected in formal caregiving situations. Parents are likely to invite caregivers to family gatherings and celebrations. Although not attending would not usually be viewed negatively, attending such events may enhance the positive communicative relationship that is so important in a caregiving situation.

The Challenge of Diversity

An unfortunate social circumstance often reported in caregiving situations with bilingual and non-English-speaking children is the caregiver's tendency to perceive the children and their families as foreigners. The noticeable fact that the children and their families usually do not speak English marks them as "different," and this observed difference sometimes leads to the caregiver's negative feelings and treatment, perhaps stemming from a sense of defensiveness and suspicion. Such uncomfortable social situations often lead to the caregiver's desire to change the difference by ridding children and their families of those attributes that make them different. Unfortunately, such

attempts arouse only suspicion and negative reactions from the infants and their families. Rather than attempt to minimize diversity, everyone can enrich his or her life by appreciating and respecting the diversity.

Appreciating the significance and validity of the child's and family's language and culture is a challenge in itself. But today, when such a large number of children from diverse language and cultural groups are experiencing early child care, that appreciation must be transformed into challenging actions that go beyond acknowledging diversity. Having caregivers from the cultural and linguistic backgrounds of the families in need of child care is important. If the child care program staff is unable to communicate with the child and family in their home language, whenever possible the staff should refer the family to a program that can.

Meeting the challenge of language and cultural diversity creates conflict, some of it inevitable and some of it unnecessary. Attitudes of condescension can be viewed as a signal to children and their parents to abandon their language and culture in favor of English and the mainstream culture. Caregivers who emphasize the mainstream values pull children away from the important linguistic and social resources available in the family and community. As a result, some parents may become wary of placing their children in caregiving situations that do not emphasize and practice their own values, traditions, and language. Other parents may come to believe that only if they abandon their language and culture will their children succeed in American society. A family's rich cultural heritage should not be robbed because of anyone's insensitive attitude and incorrect understanding about language development.

The obvious solution to this predicament seems simple: ensure that caregivers come from representative linguistic and cultural groups and utilize their personal and professional expertise to achieve the required supportive ambience so necessary for infant growth and development. In many caregiving situations, however, this simple solution is not yet possible. In those programs whose caregiving staff does not represent the children served, the caregivers' increased understanding and appreciation of the linguistic and cultural diversity of the children will create a positive caregiving context for the infant, the family, and the staff.

The development and maintenance of such an environment requires the staff's willingness to set aside their misconceptions about the linguistic and cultural groups with which they have had limited contact. In addition, staff must be willing to learn from the children and the families they serve. Caregivers who serve linguistically diverse populations and who learn the family's language will be deeply appreciated; their efforts will be seen as a signal of acceptance and respect.

In today's increasingly diverse society, where minorities are fast becoming majorities, unfounded stereotypes and condescension have no place in a caregiving staff. The caregivers' commitment to and respect for diversity can be translated into a highly supportive child care atmosphere in which children and families thrive.

Conclusion

By understanding and appreciating the issues discussed, the caregiver can make providing care to infants from bilingual and non-English-speaking homes a rewarding experience. Keep in mind and practice the following:

1. Provide a secure communicative environment for all children. Remember that the goal, whenever possible, is for the child's primary caregiver to speak the native language of the family and to reflect the family's cultural heritage. When this is not possible, it is important to find some regular assistance from others who speak the family's or infant's native language. When speaking to the infant in a language other than the infant's, use your native language as a natural communicative tool.
2. "Bathe" infants in a rich linguistic environment. Provide lots of opportunities for verbal and nonverbal communication, both listening to and watching the child and responding with the voice, facial expressions, and gestures. Also use music, stories, and other communicative means that expose the child to and engage the child in a wide variety of language and communication.
3. Set aside all negative myths and misunderstandings about bilingualism.
4. Communicate effectively with the infant's family, formally, informally, and frequently, in their native language.
5. Have a great time!

References

August, Diane, and Eugene Garcia. *Language Minority Education in the*

United States: Research, Policy and Practice. Springfield, Ill.: Charles C. Thomas, Pub., 1988.

Beyond Language: Social and Cultural Factors in Schooling Language Minority Students. Los Angeles: Evaluation, Dissemination, and Assessment Center, California State University, 1986.

Binkley, Marilyn R. *Becoming a Nation of Readers: Implications for Teachers.* Washington, D.C.: U. S. Government Printing Office, 1986.

Cummins, James. *Bilingualism and Special Education: Issues in Assessment and Pedagogy.* San Diego: College-Hill Press, Inc., 1986.

Cummins, James. "Cognitive/Academic Language Proficiency, Linguistic Interdependence, the Optimal Age Question and Some Other Matters," *Working Papers on Bilingualism,* No. 19, 1979.

Cummins, James. "Linguistic Interdependence and Educational Development of Bilingual Children," *Review of Educational Research,* Vol. 17 (1979), 169–191.

Cummins, James. "The Role of Primary Language Development in Promoting Educational Success for Language Minority Students," in *Schooling and Language Minority Students: A Theoretical Framework.* Los Angeles: Evaluation, Dissemination, and Assessment Center, California State University, 1981, pp. 1–49.

Duncan, Sharon, and Edward DeAvila. "Bilingualism and Cognition: Some Recent Findings," *NABE Journal,* Vol. 4 (1979), 15–50.

Edelsky, Carole. *Writing in a Bilingual Program: Había Una Vez.* Writing Research Series, Vol. 5. Edited by Marcia Farr. Norwood, N.J.: Ablex Publishing Corp., 1986.

Ervin-Tripp, S. "Some Strategies for the First Two Years," in *Cognitive Development and the Acquisition of Language.* Edited by Timothy E. Moore. San Diego: Academic Press, 1973.

Garcia, Eugene. "Attributes of Effective Schools for Language Minority Students," *Education and Urban Society,* Vol. 20, No. 4 (1988), 387–398.

Garcia, Eugene. "Bilingual Development and the Education of Bilingual Children During Early Childhood," *American Journal of Education* (November, 1986), 141–157.

Garcia, Eugene. *Early Childhood Bilingualism: With Special Reference to the Mexican-American Child.* Albuquerque: University of New Mexico Press, 1983.

Garcia, Eugene. *The Mexican American Child: Language, Cognition and Social Development.* Tempe: Arizona State University, 1983.

Garcia, Eugene, and B. Flores. *Language and Literacy Research in Bilingual Education.* Tempe: Arizona State University, 1986.

Gosejean, F. *Life with Two Languages: An Introduction to Bilingualism.* Cambridge, Mass.: Harvard University Press, 1982.

Hakuta, Kenji. *Mirror of Language: The Debate on Bilingualism.* New York: Basic Books, Inc., 1987.

Hakuta, Kenji, and Eugene Garcia. "Bilingualism and Education," *American Psychologist,* Vol. 44, No. 2 (1989), 374–379.

Heath, Shirley. "Sociocultural Contexts of Language Development," in *Beyond Language: Social and Cultural Factors in Schooling Language Minority Students.* Los Angeles: Evaluation, Dissemination, and Assessment Center, California State University, 1986.

Krashen, Steven D. "Bilingual Education and Second Language Acquisition Theory," in *Schooling and Language Minority Students: A Theoretical Framework.* Los Angeles: Evaluation,

Dissemination, and Assessment Center, California State University, 1981.

Lambert, Wallace E., and G. Richard Tucker. *Bilingual Education of Children: The St. Lambert Experiment.* Rowley, Mass.: Newbury House, 1972.

Legarreta, D. "The Effects of Program Models on Language Acquisition by Spanish Speaking Children," *TESOL Quarterly,* Vol. 13 (December, 1979).

McLaughlin, Barry. *Second Language Acquisition in Childhood: Preschool Children* (Vol. 1). Hillsdale, N.J.: Lawrence Erlbaum Associates, Inc., 1984.

McLaughlin, Barry. "Second-Language Learning in Early Childhood: Some Thoughts for Practitioners," in *Second Language Learning by Young Children.* Sacramento: Child Development Advisory Committee, 1985.

Ovando, Carlos, and Virginia Collier. *Bilingual and ESL Classrooms: Teaching in Multicultural Contexts.* New York: McGraw-Hill Publishing Co., 1985.

Ramirez, Arnulfo. *Bilingualism Through Schooling.* Albany: State University of New York Press, 1985.

Schooling and Language Minority Students: A Theoretical Framework. Los Angeles: Evaluation, Dissemination, and Assessment Center, California State University, 1981.

Studies on Immersion Education: A Collection for United States Educators. Los Angeles: Evaluation, Dissemination, and Assessment Center, California State University, 1984.

Suggested Activities Related to Language Development for Preschool-Age Children. Sacramento: California Department of Education, 1989.

Thompson, G. G. *Child Psychology.* Boston: Houghton Mifflin, 1952.

Wilig, A. C. "A Meta-Analysis of Selected Studies on the Effectiveness of Bilingual Education," *Review of Educational Research*, Vol. 55 (1985), 269–317.

Wong-Fillmore, L., and C. Valadez. "Teaching Bilingual Learners," in *Handbook of Research on Teaching* (Third edition). Edited by Merlin C. Wittrock. New York: Macmillan Publishing Co., 1986, pp. 361–387.

Points to Consider

1. Am I providing a native-language-speaking adult for each child in the caregiving setting? This is important for the following reasons:
   - Finding another parent or volunteer who speaks the child's native language and who will spend time with the infant helps the child feel comfortable in the caregiving setting.
   - Providing support for the child's home language reinforces the child's social, cognitive, and language skills necessary for effective communication.
   - Helping the child acquire a strong foundation and capability in his or her native language facilitates the child's learning a second language.

2. Do I respond sensitively and naturally to the communicative signals of an infant whose native language differs from mine just as I would with a child whose language is the same as mine?

3. In my communication with parents, do I regularly enlist an adult who can speak the family's native language? Note that all formal, written communication and parent meetings and conferences need to be in the parents' native language so they can understand the information being provided.

Caregiver's Practices

The caregiver working with infants and toddlers from linguistically diverse homes can support language development and communication by:

1. Listening and talking with children
   The caregiver:
   - Supports all children, from non-English-speaking, bilingual, and English-speaking homes, in developing and enhancing their native language as much as possible by having adults in the child care setting who speak the child's native language.
   - Provides a supportive communication environment for the infant by responding naturally, listening, and talking to the infant, regardless of the caregiver's or the child's native language.

2. Providing appropriate activities
   The caregiver:
   - Uses language to respond to the child, employing a wide range of verbal and nonverbal communication techniques (pleasant facial expression, caring and soft touch, appropriate words for the particular interaction, and so forth). This kind of responsiveness is a universal language.
   - Pays close attention to the family's communication patterns, replicating and using them whenever possible with the child in the child care setting. For example, if the parents use touch more than spoken words when the child is getting ready for a nap, the caregiver follows their lead and uses the same technique.
   - Learns some common phrases in the child's native language and uses them when diapering, feeding, or interacting with the infant.
   - Uses language activities familiar to the child from his or her home (singing, story telling, rhyming, and chanting) on a daily basis. Again uses the child's native language whenever possible.

3. Communicating with parents
   The caregiver:
   - Communicates with the parents on a regular basis, formally and informally, using the parent's native language. This may mean finding native language professionals who speak the home language of a particular family.
   - Respects the language of non-English and English-speaking families alike, encourages parents to communicate freely with their children in the language parents prefer, and helps the parents find opportunities to learn English.

Suggested Resources

August, Diane, and Eugene Garcia. *Language Minority Education in the United States: Research, Policy and Practice.* Springfield, Ill.: Charles C. Thomas, Pub., 1988.

Overview of theory, policy, and practices for limited-English-speaking students in the United States. Focuses primarily on elementary school students.

"Bulletin on Bilingual Education," Vol. 17, No. 3 and No. 4. New York: Council on Interracial Books for Children, 1989.

Covers various aspects of bilingual education and the issues for non-English-speaking children. Available from the Council on Interracial Books for Children, 1841 Broadway, New York, NY 10023; telephone (212) 757-5339.

Derman-Sparks, Louise, and the A.B.C. Task Force. *Anti-Bias Curriculum: Tools for Empowering Young Children.* Washington, D.C.: National Association for the Education of Young Children, 1989.

A highly readable book, full of suggestions for helping staff and children respect each other as individuals and transcend and eliminate barriers based on race, sex, or ability.

Early Childhood Bilingual Education: A Hispanic Perspective. Edited by Theresa H. Escobedo. New York: Columbia University, Teachers College, Teachers College Press, 1983.

Contains chapters on childhood bilingualism, culture, and bias in multicultural curricula.

Language in Early Childhood Education (Revised edition). Edited by Courtney B. Cazden. Washington, D.C.: National Association for the Education of Young Children, 1981.

Offers parents and teachers a research-based approach to helping children acquire language. Discounts myths and offers practical suggestions on a variety of issues in language development and learning, including English as a second language.

Schorr, Lisbeth, and Daniel Schorr. *Within Our Reach: Breaking the Cycle of Disadvantage and Despair.* New York: Doubleday & Co., Inc., 1988.

A review of intervention programs created for young children at risk over the past 20 years, which states that we, as a nation, already have the means to provide appropriate educational intervention and support. Describes various methods, programs, and approaches used in working with difficult issues and dysfunctional families; makes the point that making a difference in the lives of children and families is clearly within our reach.

"Ten Quick Ways to Analyze Children's Books for Racism and Sexism." New York: Council on Interracial Books for Children, 1986 (brochure).

Lists simple steps to assess racist and sexist attitudes in books and other materials. Available from the Council on Interracial Books for Children, 1841 Broadway, New York, NY 10023; telephone (212) 757-5339.

Williams, Leslie R., and Yvonne DeGaetano. *ALERTA: A Multicultural, Bilingual Approach to Teaching Young Children.* Reading, Mass.: Addison-Wesley Publishing Co., 1985.

Outlines an approach to a multicultural, bilingual curriculum for young children, based on the collective experiences of children in a program.

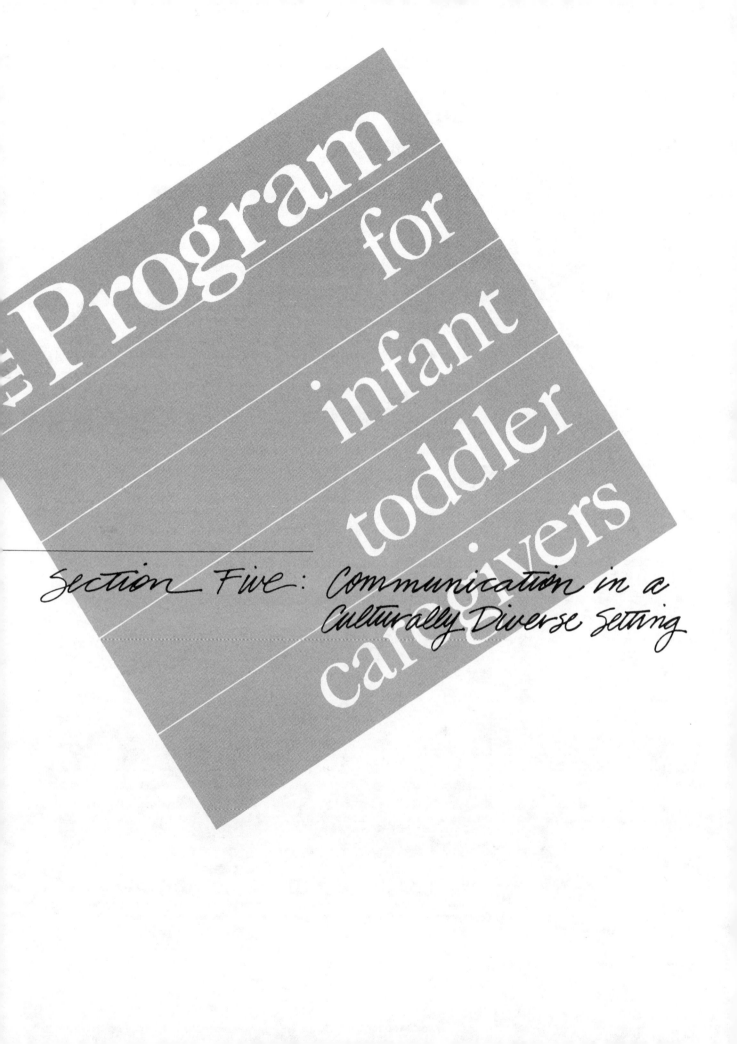

The Program for infant toddler caregivers

Section Five: Communication in a Culturally Diverse Setting

Introduction

/n this section Maria Eugenia Matutue-Bianchi and Janet Gonzalez-Mena describe the basic elements of culture that influence language development and communication for infants and toddlers.

The concepts of socialization, cultural differences, and culturally based child-rearing practices are discussed in detail. The issues in responding sensitively to a family's cultural beliefs about child rearing are explored, and suggestions are made about handling these issues with children, parents, and fellow caregivers.

Maria Eugenia Matutue-Bianchi is Associate Professor of Education, Merrill College, University of California at Santa Cruz. Dr. Matutue-Bianchi serves on many university committees, conducts research, writes, and gives presentations on language and culture and the impact of schooling on minority children.

Janet Gonzalez-Mena, Instructor of Early Childhood Education at Napa Valley Community College, has created and directed several infant/toddler programs in northern California. She is coauthor with Dianne W. Eyer of *Infants, Toddlers, and Caregivers,* which was published in 1989. Ms. Gonzalez-Mena has also written a number of articles for *Young Children,* a publication of the National Association for the Education of Young Children, including "What's Good for Babies?" and "Toddlers: What Are They Like?"

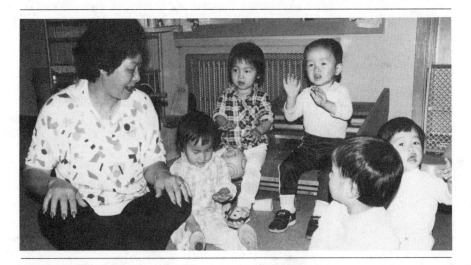

Note: This section uses many ideas from a handout by Louise Derman-Sparks entitled "How to Deal with Culture Conflicts in Caregiving Practices," First Annual Infant/Toddler Caregiver's Institute, Child Development Division, California Department of Education, Anaheim, California, August, 1989.

Culture, Communication, and the Care of Infants and Toddlers

Maria Eugenia Matutue-Bianchi and Janet Gonzalez-Mena

As we look around the world, we find striking similarities in the behavior of caregivers toward infants and toddlers. These similarities are linked to the universally shared requirements of meeting the needs of very young children. Cross-cultural researchers have identified five main kinds of caregiving or nurturing behaviors required of the adult caregiver. The caregiver needs to:

1. Be attentive to the physical and nutritional well-being of the child.
2. Relieve the child of anxiety, stress, and fear by providing emotional comfort, often given in the form of physical contact (for example, kissing, hugging, holding, or carrying).
3. Provide training for the child to achieve control over personal hygiene and bodily functions.
4. Help the child learn the culturally appropriate rules of behavior and courtesies (for example, forms of address; forms of interaction with other children, family members, and nonfamily adults; and so forth).
5. Teach the child the skills he or she will need as a toddler (for example, how to care for hunger and thirst, participate in family work and activities, sleep, play, and work alone or with others) (Whiting and Edwards 1988, 86).

Just how caregivers accomplish these five tasks varies from culture to culture. The goal of every cultural group is to produce a new generation of socially competent individuals who, in turn, will have children and socialize them in the ways of seeing, thinking, feeling, and acting considered good, just, and appropriate.

Children acquire the knowledge, behavior, and ideas of their culture from the older generations mainly through communication. Parents and other caregivers use both verbal and nonverbal communication to convey to infants information about their culture, rules of behavior, and beliefs about the world. The ability to communicate in a culturally appropriate manner is one of the many skills caregivers transmit to children. Infants learn when and how it is acceptable to talk, listen, and watch. They also learn with whom it is appropriate to talk.

As young children develop, language increasingly becomes their chief means of communication. This makes language

one of the most important elements of early childhood socialization. In other words, language development is a part of the much larger process of cultural learning that takes place during the early developmental period.

Cultural Differences in Adult–Infant Communication

In all cultures children learn language, and all caregivers read babies' signals and communicate with the babies. It is important that caregivers do so. However, people have many different ways of communicating, and their cultural background strongly influences how they communicate. Different cultures emphasize different approaches to communication. These variations are reflected in the caregiving and socialization practices of each culture.

The first three sections of this guide describe caregiving techniques and styles of communication with infants and toddlers that promote active conversation. There is a strong emphasis on one-to-one interaction with the infant that is directly *vocal* or *verbal* in nature. Through such communicational experience, children come to view themselves as capable of interacting verbally with adults as equal partners in communication. One of the goals of this approach is to make children "individual" communicators. This style of communication is prevalent in mainstream American culture.

Not every cultural group seeks to promote this type of direct, verbal, individually oriented communication in its children or adults. Some cultural groups value a person being a member of a family or group rather than being a unique individual. These cultures generally deemphasize individuality in socialization and stress the family or group.

In applying their culture's approach to early socialization, some parents or caregivers may rarely or never talk directly to babies. Instead, they may use a variety of nonverbal communication

techniques, such as physical contact, touch, facial expression, and so forth. In cultures in which this is the approach, babies are usually surrounded by family

members and friends much of the time. Continually a part of everything that goes on, the infants hear conversation around them but are not included in it except in a listener-observer role. Such culturally based experience is not simply a matter of how adult group members relate to young children; the custom also reflects what the group believes about children. For example, in some rural African-American communities, it is assumed that children will develop language when they are ready to do so (Heath 1986).

Like the infants whose parents or caregivers give them a rich exposure to language through direct, one-to-one verbal communication, infants who are in the listener-observer role receive a rich exposure to language through the continual conversations occurring around them. Instead of spending a lot of time labeling objects with adults, asking questions, or playing games, these children observe the ebb and flow of communication within a family or cultural group. They hear stories, comments, and reactions and see the rituals and traditions. These children start to see themselves as members of their group and learn how to communicate appropriately and competently in it.

Variations in a group approach versus an individually oriented approach to social relationships can be seen in cultural groups as diverse as the African-American, Asian-American, and Mexican-American communities. An example from one cultural group illustrates a style of communication that emphasizes the young child's role as a member of a family or group rather than as an individual. In many Asian families, the parents see themselves as the most important force in shaping and guiding their children to realize cultural expectations. Children must learn these expectations independently of their own personal feelings or goals. Becoming a unique individual is far less important than becoming a good group member (Wong-Fillmore 1988).

According to those who have studied child-rearing practices in a selected group of Chinese homes, learning is centered on the situation rather than on the individual because eventually children must realize and live up to family and community standards. "From a very early age, parents insist that children listen, watch, and learn how things are done before trying to accomplish things by themselves. This emphasis perhaps accounts for the differences observed in a study comparing Chinese and Caucasian infants on the amount of vocalization and smiling during the first 12 months of life" (Kagan, Kearsley, and Zelazo 1978).

The young child is taught to follow the advice, example, and direction of parents and adults. In other words, emphasis is placed on the child's actions being guided by the adult rather than the adult responding to the child's actions or questions. Because honoring, respecting, and following adult examples are more important than thinking for oneself, adults do not encourage using language to explore and understand the world in one's own unique or individual way (Wong-Fillmore 1988).

In many Chinese-American homes, children are expected to retain their ability to speak Chinese as well as to learn English. As a caregiver you need to recognize the very active role most Chinese parents will assume in their children's language learning. Although many of these parents place a high value on becoming bilingual, maintaining the family's Chinese language is seen as a most important element in supporting the child's identity and linkages to the community (Wong-Fillmore 1988).

These examples show how the child's identity, sense of group, language learning, and relationships with parents are tightly bound to the underlying assumptions and beliefs of a particular cultural group. Every cultural group strikes a unique balance between individuality and group identity. All children form a sense of identity and group belonging based on their early socialization experiences. How children feel about who they are, that is, their self-esteem, is closely connected to their communication experience with and exposure to language by their parents, other family members, and others in their home culture.

Care and Communication Outside the Home Culture

What happens to infants and toddlers who are enrolled in a child care program outside the home culture? Will they lose

their sense of identity and belonging to their family or home culture? Will their caregiver's style of communication and language confuse or upset them? Undesirable consequences for young children in care outside their home culture can certainly occur but can easily be avoided. The caregiver who is open to a child's home culture and sensitive to its style of communication can make child care outside the home culture a positive and rewarding experience for the child.

Recognition of Cultural Bias

A challenge facing all of us is *not* to judge other cultures by our own yardsticks. This is difficult because all people tend to be ethnocentric. We see our own culture as "normal" and other cultures as "not normal," perhaps even as exotic or odd. Most people consider their culture superior, a natural tendency that we, as caregivers, may not detect in ourselves as we relate to children and parents from different cultures.

As caregivers we are at risk of giving subtle messages to the child and the parent that their style of communication is bad. At times we may even insist that young children from another culture comply with our style of communication. Such messages from a caregiver, even if unintended, can harm the development of positive self-esteem in children, undermine the confidence of the parent and his or her self-esteem, interfere with the parent-child relationship, and lead to conflict among family members.

As caregivers we must recognize our natural tendency to feel superior. With this admission, we can begin to become open to cultural differences and accept the fact that the differences are not bad but simply exist. Becoming open to other cultures, especially to other approaches to communication and early socialization, means recognizing the biases our own cultural experiences have passed on to us through our upbringing. The clearer we can become about our own behavior with

infants and toddlers and our beliefs about early socialization, the more we can appreciate and respect the differences in others.

The Transition from Home to Child Care

If we view differences in communication styles as important to young children's identity and sense of belonging to their home culture rather than view the

differences as wrong, the task of caregiving becomes twofold. First, caregivers must build "bridges" between the home culture and the caregiving setting. Second, caregivers must take steps to help the children adapt to a communication approach that is unfamiliar to them.

In Section Four of this guide, Eugene Garcia explains the importance for young children, as they begin learning language, to be cared for in an environment both at home and away from home that supports their home language. If the child can be cared for by caregivers who speak the home language and are from his or her own culture, recommend this option to the parents. Also support the parents' communication with the child in their native language. When it is not possible for the infant to be cared for by someone who speaks the child's home language, Dr. Garcia suggests the caregiver learn a few phrases of the child's home language as one small way to build a bridge to the caregiving setting for the bilingual child. The familiar phrases make the caregiver and the caregiving setting a little less strange to the child. By using the phrases, the caregiver also affirms the child's home language.

Another suggestion is to learn to use a few communication techniques of the child's home culture. Observing how the child and parent relate to each other will give clues about specific features of their communication style. By using familiar verbal and nonverbal elements of communication, the caregiver can make contact with children of different cultures and help give the children the security and confidence they will need to thrive in the strange new world of child care.

Although caregivers can learn to use a few communication techniques from a different culture, they will mainly use techniques they have learned from their own culture and professional training. This is the way it should be. Being authentic with young children is important. But will a communication style that is for the most part strange to a child interfere with cultural learning at home? Under normal circumstances, it will not. Just as young children can be exposed to two languages and eventually sort them out and become competent at both, so children can be exposed to two different approaches to communication and socialization and learn to keep them separate. They learn one way to communicate with parents and others at home and another way to communicate in child care.

At first, however, the child will probably be confused. When children from a different culture are nonresponsive or appear confused, they may be overwhelmed by the strangeness of the caregiving setting. They may fail to respond to the caregiver's communications simply because the manner in which the communications are given is com-

pletely new. It is difficult for a caregiver to know exactly what is going on with the child. In such a situation, the caregiver can be most helpful by being sensitive and responsive, which includes doing the following:

- Slowing down
- Watching the child and parent interact
- Observing the child's behavior
- Discovering the child's interest or need
- Adapting to the child

Detailed information on responsive caregiving is provided in *Infant/Toddler Caregiving: A Guide to Social–Emotional Growth and Socialization* and the video *Getting in Tune: Creating Nurturing Relationships with Infants and Toddlers.*

Being responsive to children from a different culture does not mean you have to alter substantially the spontaneous ways in which you interact with babies and toddlers. By all means, play peek-a-boo, encourage infants to coo and babble,

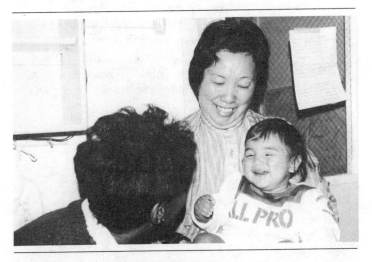

hug and kiss them, read to them, and talk to them about objects and events in the environment. But understand that the language and communication guidelines described by others in this guide reflect what could be considered normal and appropriate for middle-class, mainstream

American infants and toddlers. Young children from such a background will usually respond quickly to a direct, conversational style of communication. Infants and toddlers from different cultural backgrounds will probably need time to adapt to a new style of communication. Go slowly with those infants. Allow them to get to know you and you to know them. Together you can find a way to relate that is comfortable and satisfying to both of you.

Warning Signs

The question of language delays is complicated with infants and toddlers from different cultural backgrounds. As Kathleen McCartney and Wendy Wagner Robeson state in Section Three of this guide, caregivers are not speech/language pathologists and thus cannot diagnose language delays or disorders or suggest treatment. In addition, there is tremendous variation in the age at which children begin to talk and the rate of language development.

Cultural differences make it even harder to detect a true delay in language development. For example, does an absence of babbling in an infant at age eight or nine months indicate a possible hearing or language development prob-

lem, or does it reflect cultural differences in how parents and family members interact with the infant? Either is possible. Before deciding there is a problem and a need for referral to a specialist, do the following:

- Observe the child and parent together to see what kind of communication occurs naturally between them.
- Talk with the parents about the child's behavior and activity at home.
- Notice the child's overall reaction to sound, especially to the human voice.

This information will give some indication of whether there is a problem in need of referral or a culturally based difference in communicative behavior. Whenever you suspect a developmental problem, use these steps to determine the influence of a cultural difference on the young child's behavior.

An Opportunity and a Challenge

Caregivers of infants and toddlers from different cultural backgrounds have a chance to nurture and celebrate cultural diversity. Exposure to more than one culture provides an opportunity for enrichment. Rather than be intimidated by the task of caring for children from diverse cultural backgrounds, seize the opportunity as a challenge for you and the children to learn about human diversity.

A big part of the challenge is to learn to appreciate and respect differences in early socialization. An openness and sensitivity to the communication style to which a young child is accustomed will help you discover ways to support that child's experience in the home culture as well as relate to him or her in the child care setting. Together with the child, you can learn to communicate in a manner that makes child care a constructive and rewarding experience.

References

Blount, Ben G. "Culture and the Language of Socialization: Parental Speech," in *Cultural Perspectives on Child Development*. Edited by Daniel A. Wagner and Harold W. Stevenson. San Francisco: W. H. Freeman & Co., 1982, pp. 54–76.

Heath, Shirley. "Sociocultural Contexts of Language Development," in *Beyond Language: Social and Cultural Factors in Schooling Language Minority Students*. Los Angeles: Evaluation, Dissemination, and Assessment Center, California State University, 1986, pp. 143–186.

Heath, Shirley. *Ways with Words: Language, Life and Work in Communities and Classrooms*. New York: Cambridge University Press, 1983.

Kagan, Jerome; R. Kearsley; and P. Zelazo. "The Effect of Group Care and the Influence of Ethnicity," in *Infancy: Its Place in Human Development*. Cambridge, Mass.: Harvard University Press, 1978, pp. 217–254.

Whiting, Beatrice, and Carolyn Edwards. *Children of Different Worlds: The Formation of Social Behavior*. Cambridge, Mass.: Harvard University Press, 1988.

Whiting, Beatrice, and John Whiting. *Children of Six Cultures: A Psycho-Cultural Analysis*. Cambridge, Mass.: Harvard University Press, 1974.

Wong-Fillmore, L. "Now or Later? Issues Related to the Early Education of Minority Group Children." Paper presented to the Council of Chief State School Officers, Boston, August 2, 1988.

Points to Consider

1. Am I sensitive with all children and families, understanding that everyone has his or her own culture?

Keep in mind:

- Culture is a set of rules that defines the central core of how a person views and organizes thinking and how a person behaves and feels about all the major issues of living.
- A child's development always occurs within the context of a specific culture.
- Culture provides people with a core sense of identity.
- During the early period of socialization, the ability to communicate in a culturally appropriate manner is one of the many skills transmitted to the child.

2. As a caregiver, do I realize that I am sending important cultural messages when I interact and communicate with the infant?

Aspects to be aware of in the language development and socialization of infants include the following:

- Parents and other caregivers within a cultural group use both verbal and nonverbal communication to convey to infants information about their culture (for example, rules of behavior and beliefs about the world).
- Language is one of the most important elements of early childhood socialization and is part of a much larger process of cultural learning that takes place during this early developmental period.
- Different cultures convey different messages to young children through language and communication because each culture's beliefs, values, and goals are unique and often differ from another's.
- Infants learn to communicate through observing and communi-

cating with other members of their cultural group.

3. As a caregiver, do I recognize the natural tendency in myself and others to view our own culture as "normal" and the cultures of other groups as "not normal," perhaps even as odd or exotic?

Appreciating the cultures of other people and becoming open to other approaches to communication and early socialization include the following:

- Seeking to understand the cultural experiences and biases that have been passed on to me through my upbringing.
- Trying to clarify how my own behavior with infants and toddlers is influenced by my beliefs about early socialization.

4. Do I follow these steps to identify cultural differences or cultural conflicts in my caregiving situation?

   a. Observe myself:

   Do I identify what specific beliefs and behaviors of others make me comfortable or uncomfortable and what in my own cultural socialization contributes to my comfort or discomfort?

   b. Ask others:

   Do I find out the specifics of each family's desires for their child in my care? For example: Do I find out exactly how each family handles the important child-rearing tasks, the family's concerns for their child, and the family's questions about the caregiving setting?

   c. Adapt:

   - Do I change my caregiving practices by eliminating, modifying, or adding approaches, based on culturally important information I have learned from the families in my program?

- Do I enter into a dialogue and negotiate with my families about caregiving practices when there are differences, knowing my bottom line for appropriate and nurturing care?
- Am I flexible in meeting the cultural needs of families without negating developmentally appropriate practices for infants and toddlers?

5. As a caregiver, do I realize that I am an important "bridge" between the culture of the home and that of the caregiving setting?

6. What steps am I taking to help the children in my care who are from different cultures feel comfortable in the new child care setting and adapt to a communication approach that is unfamiliar to them?

   Do I:

   a. Use the communication techniques of a child's home culture to affirm that culture for the infant and make the caregiving setting less strange and unfamiliar to the child?

   b. Use familiar verbal and nonverbal elements of communication to make contact with culturally different children, giving them the sense of security and confidence they need to thrive in the strange new world of child care?

Caregiver's Practices

The caregiver working with infants and toddlers from different cultures can support language development and communication by:

1. Listening and talking with children The caregiver:

   - Watches parents with their infants, then uses a similar style of communicating so it will be familiar to the child.

- Notices the child's overall reaction to sound, especially to the human voice.
- Approaches children slowly and sensitively, watching their behavior and adapting the communication to provide special support.

2. Providing appropriate activities
The caregiver:
- Provides activities that are familiar to the infant by asking parents about the infant's behavior and the parents' activities with the child.
- Carefully watches the parent with the child to see what kind of communication occurs naturally between them and adapts activities to the child's preferred style, whenever possible.

3. Communicating with parents
The caregiver:
- Uses culturally appropriate and comfortable ways to communicate with each family.
- Works with each family individually in order to meet the needs of all the families in the child care program, taking into account the cultural diversity represented by the families enrolled in the program.
- Plans more than one type of parent program and communication method for reaching parents. For example, a home visit or an individual conference might be the most comfortable and appropriate way to communicate with a particular family, in contrast to a group parent meeting. For another family, the reverse might be true.
- Talks with parents about important child-rearing practices as well as family values and beliefs about their child. Discusses thoughtfully and sensitively the differences between the caregiver's values and approaches to caring for children and those of the parents. Works together with the parents to find practices that support the child and the family.
- Uses information gained from talking with and observing parents to support the infant in the child care setting, employing communication approaches and activities that are familiar to and comfortable for the child.
- Seeks out adults who share the same culture as that of the children to help interpret and guide the care and activities provided in the child care setting.

Suggested Resources

Comer, James. *Maggie's American Dream: The Life and Times of a Black Family.* New York: New American Library, 1988.

Based on the oral history of the eighty-five-year-old mother of author and child psychiatrist James Comer. Describes the importance of the author's parent's belief in education and how the parent-child relationship affects children's feelings of confidence and children's capabilities.

Comer, James, and A. F. Poussaint. *Black Child Care—How to Bring up a Healthy Black Child in America: A Guide to Emotional and Psychological Development.* New York: Simon & Schuster, 1976.

Contains advice for helping children learn positive ways to deal with racism.

Derman-Sparks, Louise, and the A.B.C. Task Force. *Anti-Bias Curriculum: Tools for Empowering Young Children.* Washington, D.C.: National Association for the Education of Young Children, 1988.

A highly readable book, full of suggestions for helping staff and children respect each other as individuals and transcend and eliminate barriers based on race, sex, or ability.

Early Childhood Bilingual Education: A Hispanic Perspective. Edited by Theresa H. Escobedo. New York: Columbia University, Teachers College, Teachers College Press, 1983.

Contains chapters on childhood bilingualism, culture, and bias in multicultural curricula.

Family Day Care Implications for the Black Community. Washington, D.C.: Children's Foundation, 1985.

Provides an overview of issues and problems confronting child care providers in the black community. Available from the Children's Foundation, 815 15th St., N.W., No. 928, Washington, DC 20005.

Language in Early Childhood Education (Revised edition). Edited by Courtney B. Cazden. Washington, D.C.: National Association for the Education of Young Children, 1981.

Offers parents and teachers a research-based approach to helping children acquire language. Discounts myths and offers practical suggestions on a variety of issues in language development and learning, including English as a second language.

Schorr, Lisbeth, and Daniel Schorr. *Within Our Reach: Breaking the Cycle of Disadvantage.* New York: Doubleday & Co., Inc., 1989.

A review of intervention programs created for young children at risk over the past 20 years, which states that we, as a nation, already have the means to provide appropriate educational intervention and support. Describes various methods, programs, and approaches used in working with difficult issues and dysfunctional families; makes the point that making a difference in the lives of children and families is clearly within our reach.

Stone, Jeannette G. *Teacher-Parent Relationships.* Washington, D.C.: National Association for the Education of Young Children, 1987.

A compassionate booklet, full of practical guidance and beautiful photographs. Focuses on an aspect of teaching that can be difficult but is essential for caregivers to do gracefully and respectfully—working warmly with parents.

"Ten Quick Ways to Analyze Children's Books for Racism and Sexism." New York: Council on Interracial Books for Children, 1986 (brochure).

Lists simple steps to assess racist and sexist attitudes in books and other materials. Available from the Council on Interracial Books for Children, 1841 Broadway, New York, NY 10023; telephone (212) 757-5339.

Williams, Leslie R., and Yvonne DeGaetano. *ALERTA: A Multicultural, Bilingual Approach to Teaching Young Children.* Reading, Mass.: Addison-Wesley Publishing Co., 1985.

Outlines an approach to a multicultural, bilingual curriculum for young children, based on the collective experiences of children in a program.

NATIONAL UNIVERSITY
LIBRARY

Publications Available from the Department of Education

This publication is a component of The Program for Infant/Toddler Caregivers, a comprehensive training system for caregivers of infants and toddlers. Other available materials developed for this program include the following:

ISBN	Title (Date of publication)	Price
0-8011-0883-7	The Ages of Infancy: Caring for Young, Mobile, and Older Infants (videocassette and guide) (1990)*	$65.00
0-8011-0751-2	First Moves: Welcoming a Child to a New Caregiving Setting (videocassette and guide) (1988)*	65.00
0-8011-0839-x	Flexible, Fearful, or Feisty: The Different Temperaments of Infants and Toddlers (videocassette and guide) (1990)*	65.00
0-8011-0809-8	Getting in Tune: Creating Nurturing Relationships with Infants and Toddlers (videocassette and guide) (1990)*	65.00
0-8011-0750-4	Infant/Toddler Caregiving: An Annotated Guide to Media Training Materials (1989)	8.75
0-8011-0878-0	Infant/Toddler Caregiving: A Guide to Creating Partnerships with Parents (1990)	8.25
0-8011-0877-2	Infant/Toddler Caregiving: A Guide to Routines (1990)	8.25
0-8011-0879-9	Infant/Toddler Caregiving: A Guide to Setting Up Environments (1990)	8.25
0-8011-0876-4	Infant/Toddler Caregiving: A Guide to Social–Emotional Growth and Socialization (1990)	8.25
0-8011-0869-1	It's Not Just Routine: Feeding, Diapering, and Napping Infants and Toddlers (videocassette and guide) (1990)*	65.00
0-8011-0753-9	Respectfully Yours: Magda Gerber's Approach to Professional Infant/Toddler Care (videocassette and guide) (1988)*	65.00
0-8011-0752-0	Space to Grow: Creating a Child Care Environment for Infants and Toddlers (videocassette and guide) (1988)*	65.00
0-8011-0758-x	Visions for Infant/Toddler Care: Guidelines for Professional Caregiving (1989)	5.50

There are almost 650 publications that are available from the California Department of Education. Some of the other more recent publications or those most widely used are the following:

ISBN	Title (Date of publication)	Price
0-8011-0890-x	Bilingual Education Handbook: A Handbook for Designing Instruction for LEP Students (1990)	$4.25
0-8011-0273-1	California Adult Education Handbook (1986)	3.75
0-8011-0972-8	California Assessment Program: A Sampler of Mathematics Assessment (1991)	4.00
0-8011-0862-4	California Education Summit: Background and Final Report (a set) (1990)	5.00
0-8011-0889-6	California Private School Directory (1990)	14.00
0-8011-0924-8	California Public School Directory (1991)	14.00
	California's Daily Food Guide (brochure) (1990)†	6.00/25
0-8011-0874-8	The Changing History–Social Science Curriculum: A Booklet for Parents (1990)‡	5.00/10
0-8011-0867-5	The Changing Language Arts Curriculum: A Booklet for Parents (1990)‡	5.00/10
0-8011-0777-6	The Changing Mathematics Curriculum: A Booklet for Parents (1989)‡	5.00/10
0-8011-0891-8	The Changing Mathematics Curriculum: A Booklet for Parents (Spanish Edition) (1991)‡	5.00/10
0-8011-0856-x	English as a Second Language Handbook for Adult Education Instructors (1990)	4.50
0-8011-0041-0	English–Language Arts Framework for California Public Schools (1987)	3.75
0-8011-0927-2	English–Language Arts Model Curriculum Standards: Grades Nine Through Twelve (1991)	4.50
0-8011-0894-2	Enhancing Opportunities for Students Underrepresented in Higher Education (1990)	3.50
0-8011-0849-7	Food Sanitation and Safety Self-Assessment Instrument for Child Care Centers (1990)	3.75

*Videocassette also available in Chinese (Cantonese) and Spanish at the same price.
†The price for 100 brochures is $16.50; the price for 1,000 brochures is $145.00.
‡The price for 100 booklets is $30.00; the price for 1,000 booklets is $230.00. A set of one of each of the parent booklets in English is $3.00.

NATIONAL UNIVERSITY
LIBRARY SACRAMENTO

ISBN	Title (Date of publication)	Price
0-8011-0850-0	Food Sanitation and Safety Self-Assessment Instrument for Family Day Care Homes (1990)	$3.75
0-8011-0851-9	Food Sanitation and Safety Self-Assessment Instrument for School Nutrition Programs (1990)	3.75
0-8011-0804-7	Foreign Language Framework for California Public Schools (1989)	5.50
0-8011-0875-6	Handbook for Contracting with Nonpublic Schools for Exceptional Individuals (1990)	8.00
0-8011-0824-1	Handbook for Teaching Cantonese-Speaking Students (1989)*	4.50
0-8011-0909-4	Handbook on California Education for Language Minority Parents—Portuguese/English Edition (1990)†	3.25
0-8011-0734-2	Here They Come: Ready or Not—Report of the School Readiness Task Force (Full Report) (1988)	4.25
0-8011-0712-1	History–Social Science Framework for California Public Schools (1988)	6.00
0-8011-0782-2	Images: A Workbook for Enhancing Self-esteem and Promoting Career Preparation, Especially for Black Girls (1988)	6.00
0-8011-0358-4	Mathematics Framework for California Public Schools (1985)	3.75
0-8011-0929-9	Model Curriculum Standards, Grades Nine Through Twelve (1991)	5.50
0-8011-0968-x	Moral and Civic Education and Teaching About Religion (1991)	3.25
0-8011-0969-8	Not Schools Alone: Guidelines for Schools and Communities to Prevent the Use of Tobacco, Alcohol, and Other Drugs Among Children and Youth (1991)	3.25
0-8011-0974-4	Parent Involvement Programs in California Public Schools (1991)	6.00
0-8011-0306-1	Physical Education for Individuals with Exceptional Needs (1986)	5.25
0-8011-0886-1	Program Guidelines for Individuals Who Are Deaf-Blind (1990)	6.00
0-8011-0817-9	Program Guidelines for Language, Speech, and Hearing Specialists Providing Designated Instruction and Services (1989)	6.00
0-8011-0858-6	Readings for Teachers of United States History and Government (1990)	3.25
0-8011-0831-4	Recommended Literature, Grades Nine Through Twelve (1990)	4.50
0-8011-0863-2	Recommended Readings in Literature, Kindergarten Through Grade Eight, Addendum (1990)	3.00
0-8011-0745-8	Recommended Readings in Literature, Kindergarten Through Grade Eight, Annotated Edition (1988)‡	4.50
0-8011-0895-0	Recommended Readings in Spanish Literature, Kindergarten Through Grade Eight (1991)	3.25
0-8011-0868-3	School Crime in California for the 1988-89 School Year (1990)	3.50
0-8011-0911-6	Schools for the Twenty-first Century (1990)	3.75
0-8011-0870-5	Science Framework for California Public Schools (1990)	6.50
0-8011-0855-1	Strengthening the Arts in California Schools: A Design for the Future (1990)	4.50
0-8011-0846-2	Toward a State of Esteem: The Final Report of the California Task Force to Promote Self-esteem and Personal and Social Responsibility (1990)	4.25
0-8011-0854-3	Toward a State of Esteem, Appendixes to (1990)	4.25
0-8011-0805-5	Visual and Performing Arts Framework for California Public Schools (1989)	6.00

*Also available at the same price for students who speak Japanese, Pilipino, and Portuguese.

†The following editions are also available, at the same price: Armenian/English, Cambodian/English, Chinese/English, Hmong/English, Japanese/English, Korean/English, Laotian/English, Pilipino/English, Samoan/English, Spanish/English, and Vietnamese/English.

‡Includes complimentary copy of *Addendum* (ISBN 0-8011-0863-2).

Orders should be directed to:

California Department of Education
P.O. Box 271
Sacramento, CA 95812-0271

Please include the International Standard Book Number (ISBN) for each title ordered.

Remittance or purchase order must accompany order. Purchase orders without checks are accepted only from governmental agencies. Sales tax should be added to all orders from California purchasers. All prices include shipping charges to anywhere in the United States.

A complete list of publications available from the Department, including apprenticeship instructional materials, may be obtained by writing to the address listed above or by calling (916) 445-1260.

90 81012   89-123 903-0278 300 11-91 5M